STATISM

IT's RECURRING CYCLES IN MEXICO AND ROMANIA

STATISM

IT's RECURRING CYCLES IN MEXICO AND ROMANIA

(Annotated)

Olga Magdalena Lazin

Copyright © 2022 by Olga Magdalena Lazin.

All rights reserved. No part of this book may be reproduced in any form or by any electronic or mechanical means, including information storage and retrieval systems, without permission in writing from the author and publisher, except by reviewers, who may quote brief passages in a review.

ISBN: 978-1-956736-85-4 (Paperback Edition)
ISBN: 978-1-956736-86-1 (Hardcover Edition)
ISBN: 978-1-956736-84-7 (E-book Edition)

Registered with the Library of Congress, registration #: TX-8-662-051 in 2021.

Tags:
1. High Schools - Statism-Nonfiction
2. Anti-statism - Mexico
3. Anti-statism-Romania
4. Autocracies
5. Pegasus Surveillance
6. Conduct of life - Genario Luna
7. Decentralization - Corporate Responsability
8. Human Rights - Russia - The USA

Book Ordering Information

The Regency Publishers, US
521 5th Ave 17th floor NY, NY10175
Phone Number: (315)537-3088 ext 1007
Email: info@theregencypublishers.com
www.theregencypublishers.com

Printed in the United States of America

CONTENTS

Introduction..vii

Ravenous Genario Luna's Trial In New York...........................ix

I. Concepts..13
        Concepts Continued..14
        Definitions...18
        The Mexican Case In World Context.........................25
        Clarifications...40

II. Cycles..40

1. "Statist" Aztec Conquest and Government..........................40

2. "Statist" Spanish Conquest (1519-1521) 41

3. Failed Anti-State Revolutions (1810-1820........................41

4. Statist "Independence" from Spain, 1821-1824,................41

5. Chaotic Anti-Statism versus Statism, 1825-1855. Includes Santa Anna's 1848 territorial losses and 1853 restoration of State control over all lands and sub-soil rights........................42

6. Active-State Legal Revolution, 1856-1866,.......................45

7. Statist Revolution under Maximilian (1864-1867)............47

8. Active-State Revolution under Juárez and........................ 48

9. Rise Of Statist Revolution Under Porfirio Díaz, 1876-1911..48

9a The Active State: Díaz (1876-1881)....................................48

9b Statism under "President" Díaz (1882-1911).....................51

9c Two Key Books—Francisco I. Madero (1908) and Andrés Molina-Enríquez (1909)..................55
10. Chaotic Anti-Statist Revolution, 1911-1916 (P. 33)............63

11. Active-State Revolution (1917-1964)..............................65

11a Political (1917-1934), especially under Presidents Obregón, Calles, Portes-Gil..................70

11b Social (1934-1940): President Lázaro Cárdenas, who confronts the World Great Depression I, 1929-1940.................78

11c Economic (1940s-1950s): Presidents Avila-Camacho, Alemán, Ruiz Cortines..................90

11d "Balanced" (1958-1964): President López-Mateos..........99

12 State-Capitalism & Dirty War, 1965-1982.....................107

12a Gustavo Diaz-Ordaz (1964-1970) Initiates...................114

12b Luis Echeverria-Alvarez (1970-1976)...........................122

12c José López Portillo (1976-1982), Petro-Statism Under the "God President"..................127

13. Shift to Active-Statism,..................................130

13a Carlos Salinas (1983-1988 and 1988-1994)...................130

13b Ernesto Zedillo (1994-2000)..145

13c Vicente Fox (2000-2006), who defeats 161

13d Felipe Calderón, 2006-2012..167

13d.1 López-Obrador, who seeks..173

13d.2 Drug Traffickers, who seek Anarchy..........................175

13d.3 Grandes Problemas Nacionales (2006)........................00

LIST OF MAPS AND FIGURES

MAP

1. Mexico On the World Globe..1
2. Map of Mexico Today..8
3. Cities of Mexico..9
4. The Reach of Mexico's Drug Cartels, 2009...................186

FIGURE

1. Top World GDPs 2009 Compared to 1999 and 1989..........10
2. How Many Were Killed, "Lost" in the Violent Phase of Mexico's Revolution?..70
3. The Painters: Diego Rivera and Frida Kahlo (pics)............85
4. Graph of Yearly Change in Mexico's GDP, 1896-19..........00
5. Mexico's Real Foreign Debt, 1964-2008............................111
6. Luis Echeverría has just been inaugurated as President by Gustavo Díaz Ordaz...121
7. Echeverría's Legal Revolution, 1970-1976..........................00
8. Norman Borlaug, who helped teach the world....................155
9. Two Alternative Methods of Making World Population Projections, 1955-2050 156
10. Human Population Growth, 1950-2050............................00
11. Mexico's GDP Real Growth Rate, 1981-2003..................171
12. World GDP Collapse, 2008-2009, Recovery for the Rich in 2010..172
13. World Oil Prices and Capital Flows, 2001-2009...............00

14. Known number of persons killed in Mexico's Drug War, 2006-2009..........176

15. Monthly Earnings in Mexico Narco War..........181

16. Calderón's Positive and Negative Drug War 183

17. Mexican Drug Cartels and Their Capos—Living and Dead, 2009..........187

18. Many-Pronged Crisis Since 2009..........190

19. Mexican Crude Oil Production..........00

20. Mexico's Real GDP per capita as Percentage of U.S. Real GDP per capita..........00

21. Mexican Heads of State Since Independence. Pouring Money Down the Rathole, The U.S. -Merida Initiative, Just Created More Killings..........00

22. Civil Society Keeps Statism in Check, Countervailing the power Lydia Cacho's Case..........00

23. Conclusion without end: Pegasus :..........209

24. Power of government in Mexico & România..........00

25. Genaro Garcia Luna, the Mexican Military, and Plan Mexico 198..........00

26. Author's Biography & Conclusion..........00

27. Conclusion..........224

DEDICATION

To my loving parents who always supported me in Romania, Magdalena Lazin, Eugen Lazin, Claudia & Elisabeta Lazin, Dr. Marin Popan, my colleague, Dr. Valeria Bilt, in Securitate infested Romania. Deep gratitude goes to James W., my mentor at UCLA, to Vice President Kamala Harris, and Joe Biden, the United States President for standing for, and with the Truth during the unbearable Covid19 pandemic. Our Truth.

INTRODUCTION

Ever since the Covid-19 pandemic was recognized by California State Governor Gavin Newsome on March 12th, 2020, I had started to compare how new laws and new regulations have come about in countries run by autocratic leaders in California, USA, Mexico and Romania.

At the time of March12, these three countries were run by outright autocracies and still in 2022, except the USA.

Fortunately, a disingenuous Trump left office unwillingly on Jan 20 after the riot he set up by sending his "mad followers" to seize the Capitol to stop the Congress from ratifying Joe Biden as President on Jan 6, 2021. Which challenged Trump's idiotic response to the major problem of pandemic.

The population of my 4 cases in 2020 where about :
California 40 MILLION persons
USA 442 MILLION
Mexico 127 MILLION people
Romania 28 MILLION people, in 2020.

My view is that there are periods in each countries, as well the "bell-weather" State of California all have faced with periods of "high central government authority" alternating with an Anti-Statist period of "minimal central government authority," and an "Active State" that "mediates between" the other two polarized points. Recurring cycles of governmental abuse of human rights had been coming in waves also in the U.S., as well as Mexico, and România.

The pandemic has, unfortunately, exacerbated the invasion of citizen's privacy by authoritarian governments, with the exception of California, and with Trump dismissed from the presidencv, in favor of Biden, the American Presidency to help save their citizens from passing Covid -19 (and its Nile Variant,) by advising their population to wear a mask and be vaccinated free of charge.

Trump and his authoritarian brethren in North Korea, China, and Russia, have done little to save people, and protect human rights, causing upheavals and the attack on the Capitol in January 6th.

There were and still are Similar attempts in Romania by the dreaded Security Services in Romania

Ravenous Genario Luna's Trial in New York

There are no checks and balances in place in the Mexican Judicial system, and the security system is not subject to parliamentary control, which makes it vulnerable to abuse, and corruption.

Genario Garcia Luna, was a spy working for the now-defunct CISEM agency before he became the infamous federal secretary of the Mexican FBI, named AFI.

During the late 2001, Genario Garcia Luna, was at the time the head of Mexico's Federal Investigative Agency, the AFI. Time when he met Guzman, and started taking bribes from him.

Garcia Luna had been hunting down Chapo Guzman starting in 2004, with the help of the DEA agents.

Through an intricate twist of fate, general Genario Luna ended up receiving huge bribes from El Chapo Guzman, and his dreaded Sinaloa Cartel. He effectively helped and facilitated the crimes of the cartel for 19 years. Avaricious, and a rapacious individual has taken the Mexican people's trust, and destroyed an entire nation, just to enrich himself, and his family.

In the span of 15 years, he had been avariciously hoarding cartel money, so that based on the prestige of his wealth and position in the Mexican power echelon, he migrated to the United States, and accumulated houses, cars, etc, letting down millions of Mexicans, even condemning them to certain death.

Genario G. L. was finally arrested in Texas, in 2020, and is now serving a sentence for corruption in New York.

Furthermore, as a leader of the deep state, Garcia Luna, working with the president of Mexico and acolytes, had obtained illegally $250 million from the Mexican government between 2012 and 2018 through an unlawfull government-contracting scheme, officials alleged in the lawsuit filed in Florida court on September 21, 2021. Those funds, and more were afterwards allegedly transferred out of Mexico using an "extensive" American-Mexican criminal network, in order to "hide the stolen funds in numerous assets" located in the United States.

Only now, has finally AMLO caught up with the General's crimes, in eliminating hundreds of thousands of governmental workers, journalists, and activists, as well as state contracts he easily obtained with corrupt party leaders. The general has used the Pegasus project to surveil the civic society activists, students, opposition leaders, in order to 'evaporate" oppositions.

The slowness of uncovering these heinous crimes makes the Mexican State, over-bloated, and partner in crimes with Gen. Genario Luna.

Checks and balances are absolutely necessary to stop these types of statist abuses to occur in Mexico, as well as in Romania, to curtail the powers of Securitate. (SRI)

MAP 1

Mexico On The World Globe

Mexico is physically about the size of today's American West that was taken from it in the MexicanAmerican War of 1845-1848—in the current History books.

By total area (858,000 sq. miles), Mexico is the 14th largest nation in the world, excluding the European Union (which is made up of 27 independent countries, and excluding uninhabited dependent territories.)

With a population of about 128,932,753 million and increasing, Mexico is the 11th most populous country according to UN data, as of 2021.

Mexico is a federation comprising thirty one states and a Federal District, Mexico City, the country's capital, which has become in effect the 32nd state, is now called CDMX, which stands for Ciudad de MX.

By contrast, Romania's population in Eastern Europe is estimated at 19,237,691, and decreasing România ranks number 61 in the list of countries by population. Romania has 32 administrative counties.

Since 1994 Mexico has been the Latin American member of the Organization for Economic Cooperation and Development (OECD). However, in January 2010 Chile will become the second Latin American member, provided that its (or when) its investment and tax policies meet OECD standards. The OECD is based in Paris and its 30 members must meet first world s tandards t o b e i nvited a nd eligible to join.

Why Mexico and Romania? Because the two states had been experimenting with statism, and state corporatism, which is a entrenched political culture closely related to fascism, during the Nazi occupation in Europe. The adherents to this type of societal organization hold that the corporate group which cements the nation together is the state. They then coalesce into economic interest groups, to join an officially detached interest group, which participate in policymaking. Consequently, the state has a great reach, and controls all the public corporate groups, and groups have great control over their members.AMLO has coalesced one.

Statism Defined

I need to first of all acknowledge my scientifically charged years at the University of Babes Bolyai in Cluj, Romania during the post coup d'état in December 1989. I graduated in 1992, in July, in Philology, and I had my fair share of statist education, which I repudiated since.

I lived for 30 years, and been raised in a statist country, surrounded by more statist, and socialist countries, and I know how planned economies are run. Socialist states are nothing but milk cows for failed leaders, corrupt businessmen, and laboring masses, who sustain this type of clans.

Romania has politically experimented for 40 years with corporatism closely related to fascism under Nicolae Ceausescu, the dictator's rein since 1953 to 1989, when a coup d'etat took place.

I know Mexico better than my country of origin, due to the knowledge of the Napoleonic Code, that is the justice model, based on Roman Law. I have written about the HABEAS CORPUS in the USA, and the Mexican AMPARO, and how they compare. You can find this study on scribd.com.

In Mexico, which I studied deeply, and have done 30 years of research at UCLA in the History department, where I earned my doctoral degree, I have recognized, and seen the ironies and complexities of Romanian statism, and this is how this book was born. I hereby thank my mentors, Professor James W Wilkie, and Carlos Alberto Torres, with whom I did the angling on these complex issues, and helped me put this pieces of puzzle together.

"Statism" occurs anywhere when the State Central Government controls a big part, usually over 50% and in some cases all of the national economy. Under the guise of statism, interest groups, are yielding corporate power over major industries that are of "strategical importance", analogue to and similar to fascism, and its grip on economic power during the 3rd Reich.

Destatification is the opposite of this process, and strong leadership can undo the state corporativist system, with the elimination of interest groups and their grip on the nationalistic economy, present at different times both in Mexico, and Romania.

These are the cycles and trends that we are focusing on in these 22 Chapters. Both Mexican and Romanian leaders have experimented with statism for decades, much to their advantage, and the detriment of their nations.

Leaders who follow statist policies claim to operate in the name of the "people". Theoretically individuals are more important than the State, but the reverse is true.

Statism is accompanied by full or major control of politics and society (not easily quantified), resulting in predatory dictatorship making decisions through partial or full Central Planning. Civil Sector Police, military, legislators, and judicial officials follow orders.

The masses are expected to take orders from their supreme leader and his regional and local bosses, doing so without argument. In Mexico the local bosses are called "caciques". Government may be based on "State Capitalism," as in today's China and Russia.

Aspects of Statism include control of tariffs to "protect" the national economy, permissions to favorite persons or labor unions (syndicates) to monopolize companies that produce energy (oil, electricity), newspapers, television, and telephone systems, while watching for suspicious persons.

Statism allows for uncontrollable surveillance of its citizens (like the NSA in the USA does.) In Mexico governmental surveillance tools are being abused and misused for personal gain.

Statist systems tend to develop "One Party Democracies" or "Official Parties" to justify (often through fraudulent elections and/or the purchasing of votes) for the purpose of remaining in "permanent "control of the Government.

Even nowadays, in 2021, Manuel Lopez Obrador, operates on the statist model of development, which is a myth and a failure demonstrated by the history of Mexico. Airport contracts are being awarded to the military officers high up in the ranks, without any regards to safety, and equity.

His train, and train rails plan for modernizing the routes taken by the indigenous peoples in the mountains has also failed, for lack of realistic infrastructure planning. AMLO's USMCA is not working.

Civic Society is based in NonProfit Foundations and community organizations that hold accountable Civil Society (which includes Government Offices, Military, and Police) as I mentioned in La Globalización se Descentraliza: Libre Mercado, Fundaciones, Sociedad Cívica y Gobierno Civil en las Regiones del Mundo, Universidad de Guadalajara, UCLA Program on Mexico, PROFMEX WORLD, CASA JUAN PABLOS EDITOESL, 2007, especially pp. 190-191:

http://www.profmex.org/ciclosytendencias/vinculos/resa36x.php For a different view of "Statism," see, for example, "The Gl obal Race to Reinvent the State," by John Micklethwait and Adrian Wooldridge, Penguin Press, 2014.

Moving into the 20th century, Mexico is the only country to have an FTA with both NAFTA, now titled USMCA (a free trade agreement between the United States, Canada, and Mexico Trade Agreement) and the European Union. USMCA has been signed by the notoriously antiMexican president Donald Trump, in conjunction with López Obrador, and Justin Trudeau, in 2020. In 2021, in an effort t o coalesce in eliminating tariffs, leaders have a an improved Free Trade Agreement, renamed USMCA (USA, Mexico and CANADA) which is an improvement over NAFTA (signed in 2000 by Bill Clinton and Ernesto Zedillo), in that environmental protections were finally included for all three member countries.

As free, and managed trade agreements progress among the three countries, the problem is Lopez Obrador (AMLO for short), would not discuss the terms of NAFTA 0.2 with President Joe Biden, because of his loyalty to criminally charged exUSA President Donald Trump, who was twice impeached this year because of his lighting up the fuse with fire, and for the ransacking of the US Capitol on January 6th, 2021.

Despite harnessing the sentiments of nationalism in QAnon types, in America, Donald Trump has failed miserably in signing the USA, Mexico, and Canada agreement (USMCA), or NAFTA 2.0 1st of January, 2021. The labor laws are now treating Mexicans unfairly.

AMLO is not inspecting planes properly, and Mexico's airline carriers and aviation, and consequently Mexico's airsafety rating had been downgraded as of May 25th, 2021.

He is spending the money on the rails and trains around the Yucatan.
Mexicans navy controls all the ports (where imports and exports are going through. it has no plans, and the officers are only getting richer.

The Mexican navy officers are just running the navy for themselves, they protect Lopez Obrador, and his crowd, in order to make themselves rich, by kissing up to the actual president (Corporativists)

U.S. Vice President Kamala Harris is supposed to work out a better USMCA deal, on June 7th, on e day after the elections.

SOURCE: Thehill.com (may 24, 2021).
Drawn from James W. Wilkie, ed. Statistical Abstract of Latin America (SALA Vol. 38, Los Angeles: UCLA Latin American Center Publications, 2002) as well as upon http://en.wikipedia.

org/wiki/Mexico and http://businesswithlatinamerica.blogspot.com/2009/12/chile is-becoming-oecd-member-in.html See also PROFMEX, Consortium for Mexico Group on Facebook.

MAP 2

MEXICO PHYSICAL MAP
THE PHYSICAL MAP SHOWS RAIL ROUTS

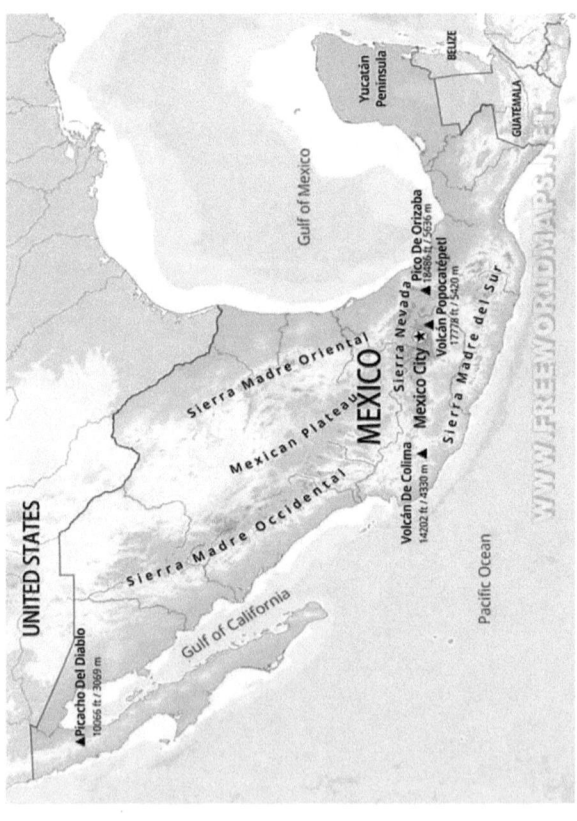

MAP 3

MEXICO AND ITS MAJOR CITIES TODAY

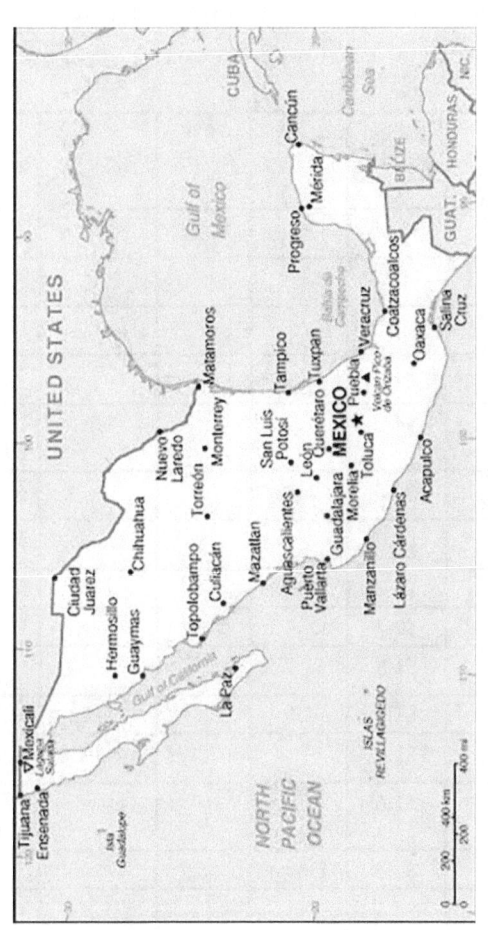

Source: www.mexonline.com/maps/pics/map-of-mexico.gif

Top World GDPs.* 2009 Compared to 1999 and 1989

(In Billions of of 2009 Dollars, U.S. GDP = $14.3 Trillion Dollars; Mexico GDP = $1.2 Trillion Converted at Market or Government Official Exchange Rate)

2009 RANK	Trillion RANK GDP	Rank Change	1999 RANK	Rank Change	1989 RANK
WORLD	$62.3				
EU	$18.9				
USA	$14.3		1		1
JAPAN	$4.8		2		2
CHINA	$4.2	UP	7	UP	11 In 2009 = 29% of U.S.
GERMANY	$3.8	Down	3		3
FRANCE	$3.0		5	Down	4
UK	$2.8	Down	4	UP	6
ITALY	$2.4	Down	6	Down	5
CALIF.	$1.8				
RUSSIA	$1.8	UP	21	Down	8
SPAIN	$1.7		9	UP	10
BRAZIL	$1.6		10	Down	9 In 2009 = 29% of U.S. GDP
CANADA	$1.5	Down	8	Down	7
INDIA	$ 1.2		12	UP	13 Mexico is #12? (See note Mexico)
MEXICO	$1.2	Down	11	UP	16 In 2009 = 8% of U.S. GDP

GRAN L.A.	$1.1++				
AUSTRALIA	$1.1		14	Down	12
NETHERLANDS	$1.0		15	Down	14
S. KOREA	$.9	Down	13	UP	15
TURKEY	$.8	UP	22	UP	25
POLAND	$.6	UP	24	UP	30
INDONESIA	$.5	UP	28	Down	26
BELGIUM	$.4	Down	18	UP	19

GDP DEFINITION: GDP is the sum all goods and services produced by resident (domestic and foreign) in a nation's economy plus any product taxes and minus any subsidies not included in the value of the products. It is calculated without making deductions for depreciation of manufactured assets or for depletion and degradation of natural resources. Data are in current U.S. dollars. Dollar figures for GDP are converted from domestic currencies using single year official exchange rates. Excludes income from informal economy and sale of used goods; also excludes production and sale of illegal drugs—they been "laundered" into productive categories of the legal economy.

GDP differs from gross national product (GNP), which is defined to include all final goods and services produced by resources owned by that nation's residents (including foreign residents), whether located in the nation or elsewhere. Includes income from remittances sent home by workers abroad and foreign investment profits returned to the country. Excludes the informal economy, e.g., production and sale of illegal drugs—unless they have been "laundered" into productive categories of the legal economy.

+ For Mexico, if the 2009 revenues from production and sale of illegal drugs were included in GDP (estimated at 10% of Mexico's GDP or $118 billion www.havocscope.com/

mexico-drug-cartels-money-consists-up-to-10-percent-of-gdp/), that would give Mexico a total GDP of $1,300 billion (and change its rank to #12, displacing India. This figure is for illegal drug revenues smuggled into Mexico from sales to 20 million U.S. drug users. DEA estimates the total cash smuggled is $39 billion. On widespread use of cash, seewww.nytimes.com/2009/12/26/ world/americas/26laredo. html and (for problems calculating Mexico's total GDP, see "Does GDP Distort Mexico's Economic Performance?" (1998): http://www.jstor.org/ pss/1061214

David Luhnow, Wall Street Journal, 12-26-09,: quotes for 2009 the WHOLESALE price for one kilo of cocaine as follows: Colombia $1,200; Panama $2,300; Mexico City $8,300; NYC $25,000; RETAIL price NYC $80,000.

http://online.wsj.com/article/SB10001424052748704254604 5746142 30731506644.html++ Gross Product of Gran Mexico City in 2005 (not comparable to years here) is estimated to have made Mexico City the 25th largest economy in the world, richer in that year than Taiwan and Iran. See: http:// en.wikipedia. org/wiki/Mexico_City SOURCE: Adapted by James W. Wilkie from the following sources that mainly quote CIA data:2009: www.photius.com/rankings/economy/gdp_official_exchange_ rate_2009_0.html1999:www.nationmaster.com/graph/eco_ gdpeconomy-gdp&date=1999-1989:www.nationmaster.com/ graph/eco_gdpeconomy-gdp&date=1989 Note that CIA, IMF, and World Bank data are essentially the same for 2008 (France, Brazil, Spain, Sweden differ by one rank in top 20).To compare the three series, see: http://en.wikipedia.org/wiki/List_of_countries_ by_GDP_(nominal) California source: http://www.newsweek. com/id/232575 (1-26-10); and the report 2-16-10 by www. theglobeandmail.com/reporton business/commentary/californias-sorry-statea-major-threat-to-us/ article1469347/ Gran Los Angeles (6 counties: L.A., Ventura, Orange, San Bernardino, Riverside, San Diego) Gross Products are my rough estimate, extrapolating from such sources as www.laincresearch.com/all/Forecast2009.pdf

CONCEPTS

Much analysis of Mexican History since 1910 has involved assessing the meaning of Mexico's "Revolution" beginning in that year, and, if there was a real Revolution, when did end:

The Official Party of the Revolution (1929-2000) claims that it Institutionalized the Movement of 1910 to rule Mexico for more than 7 decades as the "Permanent Revolution Under One-Party Democracy," which since 1946 carries the name (PRI-Partido Revolucionario Institucional); and now in 2012, claims that in the election July 1st it will regain the Presidency of Mexico

In 2000, the PRI was voted out of the Presidency and replaced without civil war by the PAN- Partido Acción Nacional, which has launched Mexico's "Democratic Revolution" under which Presidents Vicente Fox (2000-2006) and President Felipe Calderón (2006-2012) have officially recognized that the Presidency of Mexico finally shares Constitutional Power with the Congressional and Judicial branches of government (both of which had served since the dictatorship of Porfirio Diaz, 1876-1911, mainly as "rubber stamp agencies") The PRD- Partido de la Revolución Democrática claims that the both the PRI and PANstand for Private Monopoly Capitalism in favor of the elitesand that only by making a Revolution to empower State Capitalism can Mexico's people gain their fare share of the national income (In 2006 the PRD missed winning Mexico's Presidency by 0.6% of the vote)

CONCEPTS CONTINUED

In contrast to the above claims of on going processes of Revolution, many scholars see the Mexican Revolution as havingended in the following years:

1919
(when Emiliano Zapata and his "idea of land reform" were killed as ordered by President Carranza)

1920
(when Carranza was assassinated, ending major anarchical violence VIEW: http://mexicanhistory.org/revolution.htm)

1940
(after Mexico's escape from World Depression #1 through "massive distribution of landinto communal farms as well as nationalization of the foreign owned rail and oil industries" by leftist President Lázaro Cárdenas)

1940-1946-1952
(when Mexico overtly shifted to Industrial Revolution and urban development "benefitting the wealthy—not the masses of communal farmers and common workers," as articulated by Daniel Cosío-Villegas, Jesús Silva-Herzog, Ramón Beteta, Thomas Benjamin, etc,)

1959
(when Carlos Fuentes sees the Revolution of 1910 as having died after having passed through agonizing "stages of death" examined

in his world-famous novel, The Death of Artemio Cruz (1962), which downplays Mexico's Commercial Revolution and the rise of Mexico's Middle Class

1968, 1982, 1994, 2000
(years for which Donald Hodges and Ross Gandy implicitly revise Fuentes "stages of death" concept in their book "The End of the Revolution"(2002))
READ EXTRACT:
Source:http://books.google.combooks?id=Fk9JW 140bJ8C&printsec=frontcover

The year 1994
(when President Salinas changed the Constitutional requirement of 1917 so that land would no longer have to be distributed to communal farms, led Mexico into NAFTA (U.S.-Canada-Mexico Free Trade Agreement), isolated the Rebellion in Chiapas by Subcomandante Marcos, as articulated by Michael C. Meyer et al. in The Course of Mexican History (2007 and 2011).

A minority view by one scholar wo argues that no Revolution occurred in 1910 (as articulated by Ramón E. Ruiz, who sees only a Great Rebellion, which existed from 1905 to 1924) Ironically, in today's Mexico all three major political parties (PRI, PAN, PRD) argue that they are each the only standard bearer of the "True Mexican Revolution."

Two of the parties have "Revolution" as part of their name: the PRI and the PRD; and all three base their ideologies on tackling unresolved issues from the pre and post-20th century Revolutions. The current general ideology of Mexico's Presidents since 1983 is based on framework of Mixed State and Private Capitalism established by President Carlos Salinas de Gortari (Virtual President 1982-1988 and President 1988-1994), the PRI's intellectual and political leader who set the standard followed by i) his PRI successor in the Presidency of Mexico (1994-2000); and ii) the PAN's two Presidents (2000-2012) The PAN now in 2012 claims that it will continue in the Presidency but Revolutionize itself to implant Catholic values in Mexico as it moves to favor Private Capital more than State Capital while finally "winning" the "War Since 2006 Declared by Calderón Narcotraficantes, Extortionists, and Kidnappers," who do not want a political Revolution, but rather to nullify Police and Military Powers seeking to wipe out criminal activity that controls life in more than half of Mexico's 32 states.

In the meantime, the PRD (until 1988 the left wing of the PRI) has now in 2012 allied with the PT- Partido del Trabajo (which was founded in 1990 based on Maoist ideals); the PT seeks to sharply restrict the role of Private Capital as it adopts new nationalizations of domestic and foreign monopolies to return in 2012 to Revolutionary State Capitalism.

Although each of the above approaches offer incredibly important information and microanalysis to flesh out our understanding, they all miss the larger view that, since the Pre-Colonial era, Mexico has undergone 13 major Cycles of Revolution to ranging from Statism to Anti Statism, each one causing major upheaval in the economic conditions of all social classes and their political status.

Mexico faces dozens of historical obstacles to development, which recur as the country moves from cycle to cycles. The cycles usually involve change in generational attitudes that fail to realize that resolution of problems is only half-solved (if that) even as new generations wants to identify the problem and priorities as they see them:

There are the dozens of identified obstacles throughout this Schema as hindering Mexico's ability to improve the way Mexico functions domestically and interacts with the world.

DEFINITIONS

The State is the system of power that holds the "nation State" together. In Mexico it involves central authority (including police and military) that since the 19th century delegates some power to political units in the country, now 31 state governments [1] and the Federal District (which is like the D.C. in the USA). The Mexican system has three powers (presidency, Congress, and Judiciary) that have only since 2000 come to have "equal" powers (as in the USA, which has served as the general "model" for government). Mexico's political units have their own legislatures and municipal governments (as in the USA).

Although Mexico's overall model has followed that of the USA, the bureaucracy follows the French and Spanish "models," but this is changing as Mexico now begins to implement the U.S. concept of justice ("innocent until proven guilty," the right to confront accusers, and cross examine witnesses in front of judges—situations that did not previously prevail. Too, the banking and stock market systems have come to mirror those of the USA in order to facilitate flows of capital.

Culturally, Mexico has often been compared to Italy: In both countries the senses of music, art, literature, and humor have thrived, in spite of often adverse conditions of juridical and politico economic considerations. For Italy and the world, Machiavelli defined governance by deceit behind masks, a process defined for Mexico and the World by Octavio Paz as living behind false faces, which he calls "masks."

---

[1] In contrast to the national "State," governments at the sub national level are "states"— with lowercase "s".

Therefore, we can identify waves, and cycles of

  a. Statism (high central government authority) have alternated with
  b. Anti-Statism (minimal central government authority), and with
  c. The Active State (mediating between "a" and "b").

"Statism," and trends of it occurs anywhere when the State Central Government, controlling a big part of (usually over 50% and in some cases all) of the national economy (GDP), claims to operate in the name of the "people" to improve the standard of living. For the people of Mexico, and Romanian people respectively. The Romanian President Nicolae Ceaus escu who was elected in 1965, did just that, by nationalizing all industries, in orders to start socialism.

  a. Statism is accompanied by full control of politics and society (not easily quantified), resulting in predatory dictatorship making decision through partial or full Central Planning. Theoretically individuals are more important than the State but the reverse is true. The masses are expected to follow orders of their supreme leader and his regional and local bosses, doing so without argument. Government may be based on "State Capitalism"—see below.

  Politically Statism is associated to a longlasting dictatorship and "one-party democracy" to "justify" control of power, thus reducing Congress and the Judiciary to a role of "rubber-stamping" the "presidents" wishes.

  Authoritariansm in Mexico rules, as in the following three cases:

  The record for an Official Party's presidency is held by Mexico: which 79 years (implicitly beginning in 1921, when peace was restored to enable the rebuilding of a destroyed nation). Explicitly, however, Mexico's Official Party lasted

71 years from the time it was established in 1929 through 2000 when it was voted out of power.

The Official Party began as the PNR (founded March 1929, Partido Nacional Revolucionario), which became the PRM (March 1938, Partido de la Revolución Mexicana), and was reorganized as the PRI (January 1946, Partido Revolucionario Institucional). The PRI (now the Former Official Party), has high hopes of regaining the presidency in 2012, but without the hope that it can again be the Official Party because the Judicial Power and The Legislative Power have gained co-equal status with the Presidential Power. (Under the Official Party, judges and legislators followed the presidents orders.)

The second longest period of one-party rule was the USSR, which lasted (implictly, with "elections" and internal party purges) 74 years from "1917" to 1991. Explicitly,[2] the Russian Communist held power for 67 years (1924-1991).

The third longest period of rule is held by China—its "Communist" Party has ruled for 61 years (since 1949), with no end in sight.

The fourth longest statist socialist rule was Nicolae Ceausescu's rule of Romania since 1939 to 1989. His predecessor, Gheorghe Gheorghiu- Dej has been placed as a puppet president by the Soviet Russia, and ruled by nationalizing all strategic industries till December 1989. But Romanians had it with statism by 1947, when the Iron

---

[2] Explicitly the USSR was not established until 1924, but it was an all-encompassing fictitious name. The Union of Soviet Socialist Republics was an administrative arm of Moscow—the idea that it was a Union of Republics was a myth, but it did gain Moscow 3 votes in the United Nations General Assembly when it came into existence in 1946— Roosevelt and Churchill accepted the USSR, Soviet Ukraine, and Soviet Byelorussia as founding and voting members so that Stalin withdrew his demand for a total of 16 votes. See http://www.fff.org/freedom/0995b.asp

Curtain fell, and Ceausescu had started his own brand of statism, named "multi- lateral statist society."

Nicolae Ceausescu was designing, together with the Communist party, 5 years-long out-of-touch with reality planning, where all achievements were gross lies.

Finally, Romanians, and the minorities had it with statism by December 1989, and the revolt against statism, and rule by decree started and ended up in a big blood bath.

b. "Anti-Statism" is a political movement aimed to break the monopoly of inefficient and omnipresent Centrally Planned State. Anti-Statists

hope to give the primary role to the private sector, especially by selling state-owned enterprises to private individuals and establishing and/ or restoring free market economy. Anti-Statists seek to assure that former state agencies (such as airlines, ports, railways, manufacturing industries, telephone system), which have already been sold in Mexico, remain in private hands. Anti-Statism can lead to the anarchy caused by greed for power (as in the case of Wall Street bringing down the World Economy, 2008—). To break the power structure of the old USSR after the implosion of the USSR in 1991, Russia privatized big parts of its oil industry (such as Yukos Oil), but after Putin came to power in 2000, he renationalized some it (including Yukos in 2006).[3]

---

[3] "During the later years of the Soviet Union, falling oil prices, partly caused by U.S. exhortations of Saudi Arabia to increase oil production, diminished the Soviet capacity to finance its economy and empire.... Years later, during privatization in the 1990s, a new group of oligarchs, unfamiliar with the industry and disinclined to invest, were suddenly in the position of controlling Russia's oil companies. With declining production and low prices for oil, the Russian economy went into steep decline. Increases in Russian oil production, and with it Russia's economic recovery, coincided with rising oil prices beginning in March, 1999." See www.wilsoncenter.org/index. cfm?topic_id=1424&fuseaction=topics.event_summary&event_id=408132

c. "Active Statism" sees the role of the State Central Government as a mediating one. The Active State serves to bridge Statism and Anti- Statism by adopting from both to

1. own public utilities (such as the energy sector) which theoretically will be operated efficiently;
2. support an efficient and productive private sector as well as encourage joint ventures between the state (public sector) and private sectors (be they domestic or foreign). Government will be limited to the basic services for citizens (such as police and fire protection, education, social safety net, postal service, etc.) provided that they increase the well being of the population.
3. intervene in a national economy to rectify problems of the free market. This process was "validated' by the theories of British economist John Maynard Keynes (1883-1946), who in the 1930s advocated that governments intervene via fiscal and monetary measures to mitigate the adverse effects of boom and bust economic recessions and the serious, on-going World Great Depression I, which began in 1929. His ideas are the basis for what is known as Keynesian economy theory. Keynes overthrew the older ideas of neoclassical economic theory that claimed free markets would automatically adjust (for example, by providing "full" employment as long as workers flexibly adapted to the need to reduce their wage demands in times of economic crisis.

"Following the outbreak of World War II, wrote Time Magazine in 1999, Keynes's ideas concerning economic policy were adopted by leading Western economies. During the 1950s and 1960s, the success of Keynesian economics was so resounding that almost all capitalist governments adopted its policy recommendations."[4]

---

[4] On Keynes, and the article from this quote any many ideas for this summary of Keynesianism are drawn, see http://en.wikipedia.org/wiki/John_Maynard_Keynes (Deember 19, 2009).

Time concluded that Keynes "radical idea that governments should spend money they don't have may have saved capitalism."

Keynes's influence waned in the 1970s, partly as a result of excessive government regulation that had begun to afflict the Anglo-American economies by the end of the 1960s, and partly due to critiques from such economists as Milton Friedman (1912-2006) who, from his base at the University of Chicago, argued governments could not well regulate the business cycle through fiscal policy.

But, the advent of the world financial crisis in 2008 has caused a return to Keynesian economics that has provided the theoretical underpinning for the plans of such world leaders as President Obama and U.K. Prime Minister Gordon Brown as they seek too timidly to prevent World Great Depression II, through what I has called the "Active-State."

La Revolución Mexicana (1910-1976): Gasto Federal y Cambio Social (México, D.F.: Fondo de Cultura Económica, 1978).

http://www.profmex.org/mexicoandtheworld/volume8/1winter03/ 03index1.htm On debate about my concept of the Active State, see Miguel Rivera Ríos, "La Posrevolución Mexicana y la Estimación de James Wilkie del Cambio Social: La revisión de un debate," Economía Informa (UNAM, Número 314, Feb. de 2003), pp. 44-52; also: www.profmex.org/mexico andtheworld/volume7/4fall02/posrevolucion_mexicana.htmlFor further analysis of the Active State, see my "Six Ideological Phases in Mexico's 'Permanent Revolution' Since 1910", in James W. Wilkie, ed., Society and Economy in Mexico (Los Angeles: UCLA Latin American Center Publications. 1990).

Both Active Statism and Statism will use differing degrees of "State Capitalism" (as in Mexico, 1970-1982, when presidents decided to shift from Active Statism to Statism, nationalizing ever more amounts of domestic and foreign private capital on the theory that the State has "No Need to Share" profits with the private sector), or be based on the idea that the State be owner/ controller of almost all capital (as in the State Capitalism of Communist Russia and China up to 1989).

State Capitalism may involve the sharing between the State and an emerging private sector control of money and profits, as in Russia and China since 1989, and in Mexico between 1938 and 1969 as well as since 1982 when Statism gave way to the Active State.In China and Russia today the State share is well over 60% of GDP, compared to theU.S. share of about 43%, and Mexico share of about 27%. Romania's share is 40%. Statist (and some Active Statist, as in Mexico) systems tend to develop "One-Party Democracies" or "Official Parties" to justify (often through fraudulent elections and/or the purchasing of votes) to keeping the Government in "permanent power."

On the one hand the development process requires a strong legal system and ability to redress citizen complaints; on the other hand, to successfully do so requires an Active State to mediate between authoritarianism and anarchy. When development fails, a vicious circle takes place: Statism in counteracted by Anti-Statism forces. This vicious circle is broken when the Active State emerges.

THE MEXICAN CASE IN WORLD CONTEXT

Mexico has had a strong history of government Statist Centralism dating back to its foundations under the Crown of Spain, 1519-1821, a history reinforced by Porfirio Díaz (1876-1898). Three presidents (1965-1982) sought to implant Statism and State Capitalism, reducing and severely limiting the role of the private sector.

But Anti-Statists hope to give the primary role to the private sector, especially by selling state owned enterprises (such as Petróleos Mexicanos and the huge State Electrical Companies). They seek to assure that former state agencies (such as airlines, ports, railways, manufacturing industries, telephone system), which have already been sold, remain in private hands.

Statist Official Parties (in Mexico, Cuba, Venezuela, Russia, China, **Brazil, Hungary**, etc.) specialize in establishing "Public Companies" run with few exceptions very inefficiently:

Public Companies in Mexico have meant "government owned entities," a meaning that Anti-Statists have been trying to overcome since 1983 to give it the meaning used by the biggest stock market in the world—that of the USA.

In Mexico "public" means in general terms "by and for the government, which, via a vanguard of politicians and "diputados de partido" (who represent political parties, not citizens) and who administer affairs on behalf of the people."

Mexico's Chamber of Deputies has 500 members elected for 3-year terms, 300 are directly elected and 200 are elected according to the proportion of the votes won by their party. These 200 are not elected but named by their political party. Diputados de Partido do not campaign for popular votes, but do campaign within their political to be named to represent their political party in Congress. Hence the saying: "Mexico is governed by a "parti-docracy", not a democracy. (Proportional voting was instituted in Mexico in the early 1960s and has been expanded over time.)

Thus, Mexican citizens hold parti-docracy in low esteem. Parti-docracy is a major obstacle that prevents change in Mexico, which has not been able to keep up with the effective changes in such countries as Brazil— Mexico's rival for leadership in Latin America and the World.

Parti-docracy shields Mexicos Chamber of Deputies from being accountable to voters.

In U.S. politics, "public" means the broad general non-governmental populace which monitors and make demands upon the government that is accountable to voters.
The U.S. public holds government accountable in direct election of candidates.
The word "public" in the USA also includes "Public Companies" that are owned by shareholders who buy and sell in the stock markets (as compared to "Private Companies", which do not sell stock because they represent families or small groups who do not want to fragment their control).

Further, in the USA, the broad general public tends to dislike "the government," which is seen (as in most countries) to be bureaucratic, wasteful of time and money, inefficient, and heartless, not to mention rigid (as in the TSA rules announced the day after Christmas 2009 that during the last hour of a flight into the USA, air passengers get no water or Rx, babies get no bottled milk, no toilet for anyone even with diarrhea or kidney problems, no computer, no Ipod, no books, no film in the cabins, etc.).

Why has this crazy "torture" of air passengers by TSA been necessary? –The answer involves the attempt to "cover up" the U.S. government failure to catch the would be "crotch bomber,"1 Umar Farouk Abdulmutallab. Omar was not fully searched as he boarded the plane in Nigeria nor when he changed planes in Amsterdam. (U.S. authorities had failed to connect the dots: Umar's father had denounced him multiple times at the U.S. Embassy and in meetings with the CIA in Nigeria as a dangerous Muslim, Umar had been denied a visa to return via England, he boarded his flights from Nigeria to Detroit without luggage, paid $2,831 cash for his ticket,2 and he chose a seat over the wing where he sat over the planes' fuel tanks to position his PETN bomb so that it could cause multiple explosions).

Further, U.S. intelligence seems to have forgotten that bombers may not seek to blow up a flight during the last hour, but anytime— the would be "shoe bomber" Richard Reid on December 22, 2001, had hidden the highly explosive PETN in his shoes, a place which was not repeated by Umar, Reid did not try to light his shoes during the last hour of his flight but over the Atlantic two hours after leaving Paris.

No wonder U.S. citizens tend to believe that government agencies are not staffed with officials who lack common sense.

> Because of the popular tendency to see U.S. bureaucracy as hopelessly helpless (as in the case of the "crotch bomber", above), even the rare U.S. government ownership of efficient public utilities is now wrongly ignored:

> The most famous example of a successful public utility owned by theU.S. government is that of the Tennessee Valley Authority (TVA, which covers 6 states beyond Tennessee). TVA was created in 1933 by FDR to develop flood control and electrical energy as well as jobs during the Depression (1929-1941). The TVA used its profits in the public interest while keeping consumer rates low. TVA originally provided for river navigation rules and the building of dams as well as the generation and distribution of all electricity in its region, where it held monopoly.
>
> To survive the pressure on Congress to sell TVA to the private sector, in 1999 a compromise was reached that permits the private companies to serve as the local distributors of TVA produced electrical power. TVA is the nation's largest public power company. Through 158 locally owned distributors, TVA provides power to about 8.7 million residents of the Tennessee Valley.

Beginning in the early 1980s, U.S. President Ronald Reagan, U.K. [5]Prime Minister [6]Margaret Thatcher, and Bolivian President Víctor Paz-Estenssoro.[7] set out to dismantle Statism (and its Central Planning) that

---

[5] Umar concealed his "packaged bomb" as a private body-part hidden, "naturally," in his crotch—some observers preferr to call him the "penis bomber", such a bomb not showing up on the new full-body x-ray machines installed at U.S. airports in 2010.

[6] See: www.nairaland.com/nigeria/topic-373514.0.html

[7] In Spanish-speaking countries, most persons have two last names,

father's name first and mother's name second. Thus, "Portes-Gil" is hyphenated here (as at UCLA Registrar), and to show which name prevails in common use, I underline it. Some are had been promoted in rich and poor countries by Marxist oriented leaders and academics who argued that Market Capitalism had failed.

By 1989 it was clear State Capitalism having been seen to have failed to improve life for the masses, and the Cold War fell along with the millions of hammer blows that literally smashed into pieces the Berlin Wall and the myth of the USSR, thus opening Eastern Europe and Russia to consumerism in which the "workers" could demand a telephone, a fax machine, an auto, and better food and housing as they won the possibility of moving up to the middle class.

China followed in the 1990 by linking his future to producing for U.S. consumers, who were helped by China's investments in U.S. Treasury bonds that were turned into and expansion of U.S. credit markets, enabling millions of persons to buy homes as well as China's inexpensive products. World consumers would also buy in the free market what had been prohibited by Central Planning as wasteful products. Indeed, much of what China launched into the expanding free markets of the world has been cheap "junk" including contaminated goods, foods, and medicines. Consumers said: "Buy, buy, buy...."

And consumers did buy, as did industrialists and financiers, thus driving up the price of raw materials and interest rates until consumers could neither buy what factories produced around the world nor repay the loans taken out to buy, for example, autos, homes, computers, educational degrees, and vacations.

The problem of repayment of loans simultaneously arose for nations and their banks that had i) invested in the U.S. markets as well and/or ii) followed the U.S. "model" of combining into packages so called Collaterized Debt Obligations (CDOs), which mixed many good mortgages and bad loans supposedly to make "safe" investments for resale to buyers known by first name, e.g. *Cuauhtémoc Cárdenas Solórzano,* which I put in italics, who is also known in the Mexican press and here as *CCS.*

Such as retirement systems worldwide), the resale of original loans being used to grant more credit to borrowers by such countries as England and the Nordic Nations. Buyers of CDOs suddenly realized that the packages included good loans and bad loans (that had been mixed supposedlyl to reduce risk even as they expanded credit by reselling the bunched loans), and that the nobody knew how many loans were good in each package. Once a growing percentage of loans could not be repaid, the value of CDOs collapsed, along with the world economy.

The world subprime mortgage crisis (2007—) has taken at least $3 trillion out of the U.S. economy by the end of 2009. Further the Bush Cheney duo (2001-2009) took out $1.5 trillion out of the American economy to "pacify: and "rebuild" Iraq and Afghanistan. [FLASH FORWARD: Another $1.5 trillion will be needed to carry out Obama's surge in Afghanistan and to pay for the longterm medical care of U.S. troops crippled physically and mentally in those conflicts. These losses threaten what is left of the middle class after the Bush-Cheney financial debacle.]

The resulting U.S. and world financial crisis (2008—) effectively resulted in the U.S. "bailout" of domestic and foreign banks through low or no interest "gifts" to them with out any conditions—as is discussed below.

Too, Bush bailed out and the insurance giant AIG, which owing to a lack of any real regulation or "real" insurance had put together the high-risk CDOs (which did not contain all "good mortgages" that AIG had advertised) and sold them in 130 countries around the world.

Unfortunately the mortgages had originally sold been at low interest "teaser" rates to millions in the USA who eventually could not make their monthly payments, thus becoming a major contributor to the freezing-up of the worldwide financial system and causing a credit crisis everywhere. (U.S. banks are too often not sure who owns the bad mortgages that they sold as part of CDOs to investors around the world, hence making foreclosure on homes difficult and sometimes impossible and/or resale a problem.)

Lamentably, then, Presidents Bush and Obama did not establish any conditions that banks re-loan government bailout money worldwide to citizens in need of credit to buy TVs, autos, buy homes (and refinance existing high-interest home mortgages). The banks not only refuse to loan but have suddenly reduced the lines of credit previously approved for users of credit cards—effectively ruining the credit of millions whose FICO credit score falls as they "appear" to have "maxed out" their credit lines and ability to borrow, thus preventing households and businesses to complete the buy-produce-sell cycle, without which companies continue to layoff workers. Moreover, the banks have raised interest rates for late payment of credit cards to a penalty rate of 35% APR or more. (There is now the possibility to opt out of cards when the interest rates rise, but those who do so may have their monthly payments doubled.)

This reckless behavior by U.S. banks has severely damaged Mexico's exports to the USA, which coincided with the 2008 swine-flu crisis caused by the U.S. transnational company Smithfield Farms, and this in turn caused the tourist industry to collapse. At the same time, tourism had already been impacted by the rise of kidnappings in Mexico and the collateral loss of life caused by the Drug War between cartels in Mexico and their battle with the Mexican military seeking to break their rising power (2006—), as we will see below.

Thus, since taking office in early 2009, President Obama has moved the USA from Anti-Statism (which had been established for Republican by Presidents by Ronald Reagan in words if not actions) to the current Active Statism needed to save the Private Capitalism of Wall Street from its excessive greed. Presidents Bush and Obama say that they neither moved toward Statism nor State Capitalism.[8] Under the latter, the State does not establish socialism but capitalism directed by the State.

Presidents Bush, Obama and the U.S. Federal Reserve have spent, lent, and invested in banks and companies more than $2 trillion dollars since 2008, certainly the work of Active Statists.

Statist Official Parties tend to seize land from private owners, e.g., to establish "publicly owned farms":

Stalin and Mao established Collective (State) Farms (often in the guise of "cooperatives owned/managed by individual workers"; Hugo Chávez has established state-run farms as well as "community- controlled cooperatives," which are controlled by the government through subsidies.

In Mexico, the idea of the rural land owned by communities in the form of Ejidos (Communal Farms) has dominated thinking since time immemorial. "Ejidos" existed in different forms in Pre-Colonial Mexico and New Spain as well as Spain. Ejidos traditionally were not controlled by individuals but by the local Community Council, which would set part of the land aside for each of two activities:

---

[8] Bob Davis et al., "After the Bailout, Washington's the Boss: USA, Inc.—The State of Captialism," Wall Street Journal, 12-30-09, http://online.wsj.com/article/SB126195515647306765.html?mod=WSJ_hp_mostpop_read

a. common use of a small part of the Ejido by all families for meetings, ceremonies, education, and community decisions about
b. how farming and ranching are take place, according to one of the following two options:
   i. collective by the community, or
   ii. "individual" use of communal land worked assigned as plots assigned by the Community Council to each family, which can be reassigned to other plots if the Council so decides.

As we see below, President Lázaro Cárdenas (1934-1940) preferred that Ejidos be worked by the Ejido members as a group in

"Collectively-Operated Ejidos", but President Plutarco Elías Calles preferred that Ejidos be worked in "Individual Family-Operated Ejidos" (as did President Benito Juárez (author of the Constitution of 1857) and President Carlos Salinas de Gortari (1983-1994).

Both Juárez and Salinas changed Mexico's laws by changing the Constitutions of their time to grant individual title to each Ejidatario (farmer on an Ejido) so that could have the option to sell, rent, or work their land cooperatively with private and land holders.

Without title to their lands, ejidatarios can not put up their land for collateral to obtain loans, rent, or sell their lands, all illegal if the community councils retain their traditional control. Thus, ejidos and ejidatrios cannot buy on credit tractors, trucks, and cars or borrow to "invest" in canals to channel water and silos to store their grains.

Silos are important store crops after harvest (when sale prices are low) and storage allows the farmers to wait for prices to rise in winter. Otherwise it is the private "middlemen" who buys their crops cheaply and has the credit to build silos and store the crops until market shortages lead to higher market prices, at least until the next ejido crop harvests drive sales prices down because of the new "sudden" glut of agricultural commodities. `

Ejidatarios have long asked: Why is it that the middlemen, who buy from us cheaply, make all the money because they have silos and we do not? We sell when prices are low to the middlemen who wait to sell "our" crops when prices are high.

Juárez and Salinas used their terms in the presidency to try to break the power of Ejidos, which they deemed to be living in a communistic type of subsistence farming, pulverizing the land—arguing (correctly) that population growth is infinite while available land is finite. They saw the need to integrate Ejidatarios into the national economy as producers and consumers, thus encouraging innovation in poor rural areas otherwise dependent upon credit from the central government—credit always too little and too late, if even arriving.

These matters related to land ownership in Mexico have generated Three "Legal" Land Reforms—in this case "reform" meaning "Revolution" in which the masses see their life turned upside down as each Reform eventually reaches them. In Mexico (and in many developing countries) these "Revolutions" in land tenure have been seen in positive terms by elites and folk when each benefited—seen in negative terms by those who did not "benefit." Usually elites and folk did not benefit simultaneously.

"Revolution" is defined differently by the general publics of Mexico and the USA. Mexicans, living in a "partially developed" nation, have tended to see change coming through "Revolution";

Americans[9] tend to see change coming through "evolution." Thus, Mexicans tend to view Political Revolution as involving long-term traumatic upheaval to attain economic and social change, but most Americans tend to view Political Revolutions as being only involving short-term upheavals that can then enter into long-term evolutionary social and economic change.

But what is "Evolution"? As early as 1937 the International Encyclopedia of Social Science carried articles positing that Revolution and Evolution are two sides of the same "coin", evolution being caused by spontaneous "Mutation" (the biological term for "Revolution").

In recent times, the revolution in plant and human genetics has been able to cause controlled "Mutations" (always the goal of those undertaking quick, short-term political revolutions). Thus Norman Borlaug, who spent over fifty years cross-breeding plants in Mexico to create the First and Second "Green Revolutions" for the world, supports the development of GMOs (genetically modified organisms) as doing efficiently what he previously had to do inefficiently by transferring whole gene pools rather than specific ones.

---

[9] The USA is the only nation in the world with "America" in its name, hence the use here of the terms "America" and "Americans". (Some Latin Americans feel that they too are "Americans" because they live in Central and South America, but that usage is irrelevant to how the world is divided into nations. In Mexico (part of North America), the USA generally is called (erroneously) "North America," as if Canada does not exist. Indeed, in this epoch of the North American Free Trade Area (NAFTA), Mexicans, Canadians, and Americans are all "Norteamericanos" living under the framework for economics relations for trade and finance (including international treaties that govern banking, investment, and taxes).

¹⁰DNA researchers into manipulation of genes to cause Mutations that can reverse disease, rebuild lost nerves, tendons, and limbs as well as immediately save lives, have show that Mutations may take centuries, decades, months, and now made to occur with immediate spontaneity.¹¹

Ironically, Americans do use such terms as "Industrial Revolution" and "Information Revolution", the former taking a century from 1750 to 1850. The Information is often only thought of as having occurred through the Internet since the 1970s, but this is only the Second Information Revolution. The First occurred during the spread in the 19th century of postal and telegraph services as well as railroad communication all of which have been complemented by such 20th century contributions such as copying and fax machines, Fedex/overnight mail and the telephone (radio and land line phones as well as the cell phone revolution now sweeping the world.) Parts of these Revolutions took long periods to be successful; the Internet Revolution only decades, and the cell phone has leap-frogged to become a Fast-Track Revolution since 2000.¹²

---

10 See Norman E. Borlaug (who won the 1970 Nobel Prize for having made the First Green Agricultural Revolution possible), "Science vs. Hysteria" (Wall Street Journal, January 22, 2003), for an example of his rebuttal to some groups who argue against "Frankenstein GMO Foods"—a concept that Borlaug sees as trying to make persons hysterical and fearful. See: http://online.wsj.com/article/0,,SB1043197517247186584,00.html

11 For new analysis of how a spontaneous Mutation created the gene for colon cancer in one family coming to the New World in the 1630s (the gene then spreading to the world), see Thomas H. Maugh II, "Early U.S. family passed down gene blamed for many colon cancer cases," Los Angeles Times, 1-5-2008, www.latimes.com/news/ science/la-sci-colon5jan05,1,2270853.story

12 See http://inventors.about.com/library/weekly/aa070899.htm

Mexicans go beyond the above to use "Revolution" broadly to cover the recurring abrupt change in direction of political, economic, and social policy, as is seen in this Schema.

CLARIFICATION

1. In this course we seek to find the "invisible patterns" that help us to understand "visible history", which is found through interdisciplinary analysis of economics, politics, sociology/anthropology, religion, military history, psychohistory, folklore (followerlore), Elitelore (lead- erlore), etc. Thus, we seek to discover invisible patterns by examining the same people and events over-and-over again from different angles and vantage points in time.

   This Schema offers a Linear Overview to put the lectures into context. Some lectures are Linear and some are Nonlinear (Curvilinear).

   This overview is not complete but rather suggestive of some of the themes that are developed in this course. Thus, we have here a frame work from which to delve into multiple issues that are not taken up here.

   Because the emphasis here is on politics and socio-economic matters, analysis may seem more negative than if Mexico's rich culture were the focus.

2. Last Names of persons in Latin America and other parts of the world usually combine the fathers' last name and the mother's last name, thus Vicente Lombardo-Toledano hyphenated here and by the UCLA registrar so as not to confuse the father's last name as a middle name) officially gives the father's name first and the mother's name second, but each person may choose either last name for common usage. Vicente is often called "Lombardo" but not "Toledano."

II.
CYCLES: FOR ANALYZING TYPES OF STATISM

(Like any scheme, there are exceptions to the following stylization.

In each period new problems and obstacles to development were identified in their own time but either ignored or only partly resolved, often because they were only partly resolved and because new generations did not follow through on the "old" when new ones were being identified.

Thus, Mexico continues to face a series of accumulating, misunderstood and/or partially "resolved" problems and obstacles that are "rediscovered" again and again.

This outline offers the framework into which lectures will fit many historical aspects and persons not listed here.)[13]

---

[13] For alternative chronologies, see www.indiana.edu/~jah/mexico/mapstime.html and www.cidac.org/vnm/libroscidac/underZedillo/apendixa.PD.F.

THE CYCLES

1. "Statist" Aztec Conquest and Government prior to 1521. In Nahua times, the Aztecs set up a system wherein THE leader ruled without any questions and certainly without any democracy. But, communities had local caciques (bosses) to carry out orders and also moderate demands and/or inflict the caciques own demands. Population of Central Mexico reached 25 million by 1519, a total not reached again until early 1950.

(Data on population given here represent estimates, depending on sampling by different agencies except for censuses which are sometimes more inclusive, and vary by methods, including periods of years, seasons of year, and population living/working in the USA— often many millions since 1910).[14]

(All population data presented here are from: James Wilkie, Booklet of Charts on Mexican History; James Wilkie, ed. Statistical Abstract of Latin America (SALA), Vol. 38, Table 513 (2002); and U.N. population series. Compare the preceding to research by Robert McCaa, who examines differing views of population statistics for Mexico and delves into data by race/ethnicity and by region. [15])

---

[14] For example, Meyer-Sherman-Deeds suggest that the total was 30 million, which was not reached again until early 1955, according to series in Wilkie, ed. SALA, Table 514.

[15] Robert Macaa, "The Peopling of Mexico from Origins to Revolution [in 1910]" (1997), www.hist.umn.edu/~rmccaa/mxpoprev/cambridg3.htm

2. "Statist" Spanish Conquest (1519-1521) and Government after 1521. During the Colonial Period (1521-1821), the Spanish substituted their Statist System on top of the defunct system of "Aztec Statism," and the Spanish did so under a series of Viceroys, who ruled as the "alter ego" of the far away King of Spain.

    New Spain administered for the Spanish State all land (and everything under the surface) as well as all economic production, but granted rights and licenses to a favored view to exploit those rights. Local officers moderated demands made by the Crown and Vice-roys by promising to obey without complying ("Obedezco pero no cumplo"), and the latter often inflicted demands of their own. Town Councils existed but (in contrast to the 13 American Colonies), the Councils were not democratic and did not represent or allow citizen input beyond the key elite.

    Population disastrous decline caused by introduction of European diseases, wars, and "enslavement" of much of the Indigenous population saw the total fall to 17 million by 1532 and to 1.1 million in 1608—the low point.[16] The population then regained impetus to reach 6.1 million by 1810.

3. Failed Anti-State Revolutions (1810-1820), which sought Independence from Spain. Independence was defeated by the Spaniards living in Mexico who successfully saved themselves from having their property and wealth seized in the anti-Spanish fervor. Although the Spaniards (who dominated politics, economics, and society) temporarily "won," they had to live in a decade of chaotic years.

4. Statist Independence from Spain, 1821-1824 to Maintain Status Quo. Independence was achieved from Spain in 1821 when conservatives, who had fought against

---

[16] In ibid, MaCaa estimates that the population fell only as low as 4 to 5 million.

independence from Spain (1810 to 1820), turned in favor of Independence to save the Statist system, which was under attack in Spain itself.

When Napoleon I had taken control of Spain and placed his elder brother Joseph Bonaparte on that country's throne (1808-1813), as his armies passed through to invade Portugal, the Spanish town councils of Spain and the New World finally had gained real importance when, ironically, they had refused to pledge allegiance to a French king. By 1812 the town councils of Spain had formulated a new Anti- Statist Constitution, and when they sought to implement it in 1821, the Spaniards in Mexico (who also controlled Central America) realized that they themselves had to declare Independence from Spain in order to save their power based on Statism.

The population of Mexico in 1823 stood at 6.8 million.[17]

5. Chaotic Anti-Statism versus Statism, 1825-1855. Period is characterized by:
Anti-Statists seeking Decentralization of power to the Provinces versus Statists in Mexico City seeking Centralization of power in the capital city.
Both groups successfully drove most of the educated and technically skilled Spaniards out of Mexico, leaving it by 1829 without the expertise necessary to keep the country as a functioning economic system.
The result effectively brought about chaos as the Statist system collapsed in continuing on going battles between generals who sought to become the Napoleon of Mexico, each attempting without success to install a Napoleonic

---

[17] In ibid, the estimate is that population was about 6 million.

Statist system of a highly centralized government, which seemed stronger than it turned out to be in fact.

> [FLASH TO 19th-Century FRANCE,[18] about which Michel Gurfinkiel writes that from 1830 ... to 1905, France passed through no less than four different constitutions; three dynasties (the Bourbons, the Orléans and the Bonapartes); two republics; three revolutions (1830, 1848 and 1870); one coup that worked (Louis-Napoleon Bonaparte's in 1851) and two that were either merely attempted (in 1877) or fantasized (in 1889); two civil wars (the June crisis in 1848 and the Commune in 1871); one disastrous defeat to a nascent Germany (1870) that led to the momentary occupation of more than one third of the country; two major financial scandals, in 1873 and 1892, that swept away most upper and middle-class savings; and, finally, a turn-of-the- century judicial scandal ... that prompted a far-reaching law in 1905 mandating the separation of church and state.]

Hopes to stop anarchy by imposing order were dashed by two facts the new Republic of Mexico assumed all the debts of New Spain and the country started out in unstable poverty; and b) the Presidency changed hands 36 times between 1833 and 1855, the average term lasting about 7.5 months. To survive, Presidents had to re-impose import taxes that had been abandoned at Independence, establish sales taxes, and sell monopolies to the private sector (as the Crown had done). Import taxes caused the expansion of

---

[18] Frederick Brown tells this story of that tumultuous era in For the Soul of France (2009). http://online.wsj.com/article/SB10001424052748704094304575029143722 403852.html

smuggling and bribery, sales taxes were circumvented, and monopolies could not generate profits to share with the government in the form of income taxes.

This struggle was especially influenced by Statist Antonio López de Santa Anna, who occupied the Presidency eleven times between 1833 and 1855. As a general of the army, he had led Mexican troops (a) to victory at Tampico in 1829 where he defeated Spain's attempt to force Mexico back into colonial status; and (b) to defeat in the War with Texas (1835-1836).

Santa Anna restored State power over all lands and subsoil rights in 1853, but lost half of Mexico in his war with the USA, 1845-1848. He was in and out of power so often during his 22 years a major influence in Mexico that he could not establish any long-term stability or Central Government Power.

Nevertheless, Santa Anna's Recentralization of land rights under the power of Mexico City marks the:

First of Three "Legal": [19] Land Reforms. Santa Anna's First Legal Land Reform would provide the major rationale for regulation of land in the Constitution of 1857 and the re-interpretation of that Constitution of 1857 by the

---

[19] See Rosario Varo Berra, La Reforma Agraria en México Desde 1853: Sus Tres Ciclos Legales. (Guadalajara, Los Ángeles, México: Universidad de Guadalajara, UCLA Program on Mexico, PROFMEx, Juan Pablos Editor, 2002). Prólogo de James W. Wilkie. Legal changes may not be fully carried out all, but they provide the framework of governance that creates rural insecurity about who owns what, thus discouraging investment in infrastructure, irrigation, etc.

dictator Porfirio Díaz. Porfirio transferred 32% of Mexico's land surface into huge haciendas.

The Second Legal Land Reform would take place with the writing of the Constitution of 1917, which reiterated Santa Anna's argument that the State controls all land rights (including those above and below ground) and clarified the land regulations as adopted by Juárez in the Constitution of 1857 to prevent the rise of new haciendas—Juárez had failed to "outlaw" the rise of new haciendas to replace the ones he broke up. The Constitution of 1917 required distribution of land to communities, not individuals. Land collectively held cannot be put up for collateral to obtain loans, thus was dependent for credit on the government, which had little or no money for agricultural credit.

The Third Legal Land Reform would take place in 1992, when Salinas won revision of the Constitution of 1917 to provide for granting ownership of title to the land currently being worked by a family, thus ending complete control over the land that had been held by Community Councils. Further, this new law stated that although land distribution to Ejidos could continue, it did not require it.

6. Active-State Legal Revolution, 1856-1866, established by Benito Juárez and his Chief Minister Sebastián Lerdo de Tejada was undertaken to develop the Reform Laws that were then written into the Constitution of 1857. Here are the provisions of the Constitution of 1857:
    - establish civil power to take registration of birth, marriage, and death from the Church (including taking over the Church's hospitals and orphanages, but without the funds to do so, led to the closure of many and health/social disaster for the poor),

- establish a sound market economy based on weights and measures consistent throughout Mexico,

- break up the Indigenous Communal Farms (Ejidos, many held trust by the Church) as well as large haciendas/latifundia controlled by the Church and absentee private-land owners) to distribute it to Small- and Medium-Size Property Owners.

Latifundia/Haciendas are defined as

a. huge estates larger than 2,500 acres or
b. estates not used "productively"—that is not used at all, especially prior to the mid-twentieth century. Problems not foreseen by the Juárez Land Laws: Productivity requires the normal practice of letting land "rest" in order to prevent depletion of soil health and to recover from heavy use or failure to rotate crops. Often if is difficult to know if land is not being used or "resting". Many persons see such land being "wasted" unless it is divided and distributed to the poor, failing to understand that the consequence tends to create minifundia.

Minifundia are undersized plots of land that barely provide subsistence agriculture and largely force inhabitants to exist outside the marker economy. They are farmed continually because, if the land is allowed to "rest", the occupants, cannot survive. The method of farming is slash and burn agriculture, cutting and burning of forests or woodlands to create fields for agriculture or pasture for livestock. The burning ruins the root structure and eventually renders soils incapable of further yields—sometimes for generations. Slash and burn "farming" has caused soil erosion for centuries in

Mexico, wasting the land. Because fertilizers are prohibitively expensive, vegetables are too often grown in "night soil" (human manure, which tends to cause dangerous intestinal infections unless the vegetables are well cooked.)

Small holdings may also engage in slash and burn agriculture because holdings have been too small to take advantage of change in technology such the advent of tractors as well as plant nutrition—either organic or inorganic.[20]

Juárez effectively broke the power of the Church and private haciendas (both based on latifundia or huge areas of land thought to be underused[21]), but the inadvertent result that he achieved was to begin the pulverization of the land, thus creating minifundia (land holdings too small to contribute to the market economy that he so wanted).

The population of Mexico in 1857 stood at 8.2 million.

7. Statist Revolution under Maximilian (1864-1867) backed by French Troops, who seized Mexico City (1864-1867). Emperor Maximilian von Hapsburg, invited by Catholics and other anti-Juárez groups, came from Europe to re-establish Mexico as a monarchy the idea being to "end"

---

[20] Since the 1970s a debate has emerged which favors use of "plant nutrition" (a positive term) and not "fertilizers". However the latter term includes chemical types (which are needed but too often used without proper caution) and organic fertilizers (which are expensive). See http://en.wikipedia.org/wiki/Plant_nutrition and http://en.wikipedia. org/wiki/Fertilizer#Risks_of_fertilizer_use

[21] Although "underused" land may only be lying fallow to let it rest (constant use will damage soil fertility) much land was not even used by some haciendas. The question always has been whether or not land us underused or not used.

chaos and establish Government authority over the entire country. Maximilian tried to implement the role of civil power but accomplished little to establish order in the countryside and develop the national infrastructure. Juárez central government becomes a government in internal exile, moving from state to state in the fight to regain central power—in 1867 Juárez forces capture and execute Maximilian.

8. Active-State Revolution under Juárez and Lerdo (1867-1876), seeks to implement as well as to continue programs established in the 6th Period, above. These presidents also adopt some measures to give the State a more active role for the nation, still seeking to establish standard weights and measures and a real postal system for the entire country. (To this day, the Mexican postal system is considered unreliable and corrupt—robbing any mail that looks valuable.)

The railway linking Veracruz and Mexico City was finally completed in 1872. It took 35 years from inception in 1847 to overcome the difficult terrain of mountain ranges, deep gorges, driving rain, and disease that killed many hundreds of nameless workers.

9. The Rise of Statism under "President" Porfirio Díaz (1876-1911).

The population of Mexico grew from 10 million in 1879 to 13.6 million in 1900.

9a. From the Active State to Statism under Díaz (1876-1882). A ruthless Political Dictatorship was established by Porfirio Díaz to favor the development of Mexico as a huge enterprise loosely based on following the "model" of the Barons who were accumulating huge fortunes in the USA. (That the U.S. Barons were becoming known as "Robber Barons" was disregarded by Díaz, who saw them as what Mexico needed—"Captains of Industry".)

Chaos was gradually ended when criminals were deputized as police, who agreed to limit their corruption. He was famous for has motto: Accept "pan o palo" (bread or the club, in English: "the carrot or the stick"), enforcement of which was aided by the expansion in Mexico of the Díaz telegraph network during the 1870s and railways beginning in the 1980s.

This strong President Díaz decentralized economic power to rich regional elites; and he enticed foreign capital to build Mexico's railway infrastructure, thus finally linking the country into a unified nation as well as to export Mexico's minerals and agricultural products. To do this, ironically, e.g., he used the Juárez land laws to create new haciendas and foreign owned mining and oil empires as well as railway corridors of private power.

Because Juárez's land laws to allow the creation and/or expansion of haciendas. Juárez had divided lands to create a small and medium land owing system but did so without putting any cap on the amount of lands that might be acquired by the new owners. Thus Díaz did not have to change the law, but rather simply reverse Juárez's priority— Díaz encouraged the growth of new great estates.

Díaz and the political system that he appointed (including regional caudillos or bosses and their local caciques or bosses administering the harsh rules the masses) saw their role as enabling the Private Sector (and especially foreigner with investment capital) as taking the lead in becoming and or working with the U.S. "Captains of Industry".

Whereas Juárez had emphasized the industrial role of medium and small producers, Díaz emphasized the role of Captains of

Industry and hacendados (landed gentry) needed to develop large scale activities in Mexico both for the internal as well as export market.

The building of a real railway system mainly directed to the USA as well as Mexico City was Porfirio Díaz' way to get goods to market as well as to move police and soldiers to put down any rebellions.

Díaz's success in linking the country by telegraph as well as rail had two sides: on one hand it provided the basis to regulate order and progress of commerce to generate wealth for the elite; on the other hand, it sowed the seeds of his overthrow—the railroads and telegraph allowing dissent to spread, especially by the railway workers who crossed the border running train travel between the USA and Mexico—many of those operating the trains were members of the IWW (International Workers of the World, who called for a transborder struggle that "must go on until the workers of the world organize as a class, take possession of the means of production, abolish the wage system, and live in harmony with the Earth."[22]

When Porfirio Diaz came to power in 1876, he totally opened the country to foreign capital to build railroads, even offering a generous subsidy for each kilometer of line that was built. The rail companies not only were granted the railway corridors but also ample land on both sides of every corridor; import duties were waived on equipment and materials involved in the project, and each builder won full rights of operation for 99 years.

"Immediately United States investors jumped in, winning concessions to build the Central Line from El Paso/Ciudad

---

[22] Quote is from www.iww.org/culture/official/preamble.shtml

Juárez to Mexico City and the National Line from Laredo/Nuevo Laredo via Monterrey to Mexico City. The first of these railways was rapidly pushed southward through the desert to Chihuahua, Torreón (one of the few Mexican cities actually 'created' by the rail road), zacatecas, Aguascalientes, León, and Querétaro to Mexico City, a clear objective being to 'capture' as many of the mining centers as possible without any particular regard to the distribution of the country's population.

> The fact that the Central Railway was completed and operational by 1884 not only spoke to the advantageous conditions established by its concession but also to the relatively open terrain through which it passed."[23]

> Railways played an integral role in the Yucatán Henequen Boom (1880s-1915). Henequen (fibrous cords and twine from sisal, one variety of the cactus plant) was used to make rope to dock sailing ships as well as bailing cords to bind bales of U.S. cotton for export. Henequen was also used to make hammocks, burlap bags, etc.

9b. Statist Revolution under Díaz (1882-1911) and the rise of the Científicos Social and Economic Anti-Statists were increasingly appalled at Díaz's Statist politics, a situation which denied even the elite to share in the process of making political choices and decisions.

Porfirio Díaz never did change his Statist political stance, but did gradually shift his economic and social programs from Anti-Statism to Active Statism, especially as he began to rely more and more on the ideas of his Científico "brain-trust" as they advocated plans to advance Mexico's modernization.

---

[23] Vincent H. Malmström. Land of the Fifth Sun: Mexico in Space and Time, ebook, 2002, www.dartmouth.edu/~izapa/LFS_Title%20Page.htm

"The Científicos (Spanish: "scientists" or "those scientifically oriented") were a circle of technocratic advisors to President of Mexico Porfirio Díaz. Steeped in the positivist "scientific politics", they functioned as part of his program of modernization at the start of the 20th century. Leading Científicos included:

- Ramón Corral (January 10, 1854 - November 10, 1912) was the Vice President of Mexico under Porfirio Díaz from 1904 until their deposition in 1911.
- Gabino Barreda (1820–1881), a precursor of the group. A physician and professor of medicine, Barreda studied in Paris under Auguste Comte between 1847 and 1851 and is widely credited with introducing positivism in Mexico. Put in charge of fulfilling the 1857 Constitution's promise of secular public education by the early Juárez government, Barreda organized the National Preparatory School, the first secular school of higher learning in Mexico, which opened in 1868 and became the training ground for many of the younger Científicos."[24]

Indeed to advance scientific planning, Díaz in 1882 authorized the creation Mexico's national statistical gathering agency so that the Científicos could begin the first real collection of statistical data needed to understand from where the country was going, where it stood, and where appeared to be heading. This national project was launched, mainly by Mexico's giant in research: Antonio Peñafiel, who organized the first consistent and wide recording and compiling of historical statistics as well as creation of new data that he included in Mexico's statistical reports and yearbooks.

---

[24] Quoted from http://en.wikipedia.org/wiki/Científico

Indeed, he created the first effective basis for modern research and publication of statistics on Mexico.[25]

Peñafiel had established the first Law on Statistics in 1895, the same year that he administered the first national population census for Mexico— the population in that year was recorded to be 12.6 million. Five years later his census counted 13.6 million. In 1910 Peñafiel's census showed the Mexican population to have reached 15.2 million. In the process he was refining his scientific methods used to conduct the censuses.

The "Científicos" were effectively also Díaz's "political party" which justified his socio-economic schemes developed under Big Foreign and Domestic Capitalists.

By 1898 the José Limantour, Minister of the Treasury (Hacienda), understood that Mexico's railway system had to be developed in the national interest, not the private sector's narrow interests. He and the Científicos realized that disorganized routings prevailed in Mexico's rail system. Limantour oversaw the enactment of a General Railway Law requiring that any new construction would serve to complete a "national network rather than sponsor the building of detached lines in remotely separated parts of the country.

As a result, in the later years of the Díaz administration, the Mexican government began acquiring the majority of the shares of the Central and National Lines and fusing them into a unified company called the National Railways of Mexico, so by the end of the Porfirian period the major lineaments of the private/public Mexican rail system had been well established —the country as a whole boasting some 12,000 miles of track," writes Malmström.

---

[25] See Sergio de la Peña y James W. Wilkie; *La Estadística Económica en México: Los Orígenes* (México: Siglo xxI y Universidad Autónoma Metropolitana-Azcapotzalco, 1994).

Further in 1900 he encouraged the founding of Mexico's steel industry in Monterrey, but left it to the private sector to develop.

Because Porfirio had not enforced Juárez' laws against the Church's accumulation of capital (often through granting the right to go to heaven to the rich, who paid dearly and/or willed much of their property to the Church upon death), by 1900 the Church served as Mexico's biggest banker.

Most importantly, because Porfirio Díaz paid down Mexico's international debts, credit in Mexico was scarce and costly, even for the elite, and not available to others. From 1905 to 1907 financial panic spilled over into Mexico from (a) the 1905 Russo-Japanese War when Mexico suffered because U.S./world capital was diverted to Asia,[26] (b) the 1906 San Francisco earthquake which disrupted the U.S. economy, and (c) the subsequent 1907 U.S. credit shortage meant that many members of the Mexican elite found that they could not renew their loans and or had to repay them in an accelerated manner. Hacendados were especially affected and some began to quietly suggest among themselves that perhaps a rumored rebellion against Díaz by workers could have some favorable results—if it were limited to burning the banks and credit records, after which the workers were to go back to their slave like jobs.

When real Revolution broke out against his regime in 1911, Díaz called up his army, which, as it turned out, barely existed—it was padded with "phantom" soldiers. The generals had thought that since Mexicans were so cowed by the Díaz mystique they could become rich simply by keeping the funds budgeted for positions of soldiers who they did not hire.

---

[26] Japan surprised the world by wing this war, changing the balance of power in the Far East.

Porfirio's Rural Police, who had also grown lazy and corrupt, were no match for the angry masses, who they had repressed for so long. They tended to avoid battles by deserting.

9c Two Key Men and Their Books:
ONE: Andrés Molina-Enríquez (1909) Los Grandes Problemas Nacionales TWO: Franciso I. Madero (1908) The Presidential Succession of 1910;

ONE

Molina-Enríquez, saw his book referred to in English as
Mexico's Huge (or Great) National Problems. His thought would be influential in writing the Constitution of 1917.

"This book by Molina-Enríquez] was highly critical of the Porfirio Díaz government,[it characterized] the period after 1821 as the era of national disintegration. The book highlighted issues of sharp political divisions, recurrent armed conflicts, and periodic foreign interventions.

"The book] focused particularly on two aspects, land reform, and the rights of the indigenous people and their place in society socially....

"A well-known quote from the book is 'la hacienda no es negocio' [the hacienda is not a business]: By this he meant that the large Mexican landed estates of his day (and stretching back to their origins in the era of the Spanish conquest) were for the most part not profit-oriented but 'feudal' enterprises, that rural Mexico was therefore only partially capitalistic, if at all, and that the country was ipso facto only imperfectly modern."[27]

Wilkie's Interpretive summary of Molina-Enríquez's

LOS GRANDES PROBLEMAS NACIONALES I (1909) [28]

Problems analyzed in book:

1. Varied and Problematic Physical Geography of Mexico
2. Property Rights and Problems of Registration
3. Irrigation Problems
4. Lack of Credit Problem
5. Population as a Problem
   745 Indigenous Tribes Speaking Each Speaking Own Language or Dialect Criollos (Spanish descendents, born in Mexico) Peninsulares (Spanish born in Spain) Mestizos (Persons of Mixed Blood and Culture) Human Geography andDistribution of Food Use of Alcohol Poor Wages for Masses.
6. Politics

Problem of How to define Mexico as a Nation—Mestizaje = Key Problem of Overcoming Physical Geography to Develop Communication of Such a Diverse Population Living in Different Circumstances and Speaking So Many Languages Problem of Education for the Indigenous and Mestizos Problem of Taking Population Censuses

---

[27] Quoted from http://en.wikipedia.org/wiki/Andrés_Molina_Enríquez

[28] The book is available to download at http://www.cervantesvirtual.com/servlet/ SirveObras/01471652101247384191291/index.htm

MORE STATISM: PHASE TWO

Madero's book on The Presidential Succession of 1910 was to play the role of igniting the Mexican Revolution in 1911 and lead him to become President of Mexico from November 6, 1911, to February 19, 1913. Wikipedia sums up his history:[29]

> "Madero was born in Parras de la Fuente, Coahuila; the son of one of the wealthiest families in Mexico: his grandfather had founded the Compañía Industrial de Parras, which was initially involved in vineyards, cotton, and textiles, and which moved into mining, cotton mills, ranching, banking, coal, rubber, and foundries in the later.
>
> "Madero was educated at the Jesuit college in Saltillo, but this early Catholic education had little lasting impact. Instead, his father's subscription to the magazine Revue Spirit awakened in the young Madero an interest in Spiritism, an offshoot of Spiritualism. As a young man, Madero's father sent him to the École des Hautes Études Commerciales de Paris (HEC). During his time in France, Madero made a pilgrimage to the tomb of Allan Kardec, the founder of Spiritism, and became a passionate advocate of Spiritism, soon coming to believe he was a medium. Then he graduated from High school at Culver Academies, achieving high leadership positions. Following business school, Madero traveled to the University of California, Berkeley to study agricultural techniques and to improve his English. During his time there, he was influenced by the Theosophist ideas of Annie Besant, which were prominent at nearby Stanford University.

---

[29] http://en.wikipedia.org/wiki/Francisco_I._Madero#Leader_of_ the_Anti-Reelection_ Movement.2C_1908.E2.80.931909

"In 1893, the 20 year old Madero returned to Mexico and assumed management of the Madero family's hacienda at San Pedro, Coahuila. He installed new irrigation works, introduced American cotton, and built a soap factory and an ice factory. He also embarked on a lifelong commitment to philanthropy. His peons were well paid and received regular medical exams, he built schools, hospitals, and community kitchens, and he paid to support orphans and award scholarships. He also taught himself homeopathic medicine and offered medical treatments to peons.

"On April 2, 1903, Bernardo Reyes, governor of Nuevo León, violently crushed a political demonstration, an example of the increasingly authoritarian policies of president Porfirio Díaz. Madero was deeply moved and, upon the suggestion of the spirit of his deceased brother Raúl, he decided to act. Madero responded by founding the Benito Juárez Democratic Club and ran for municipal office in 1904, though he lost the election narrowly. In addition to his political activities, Madero continued his interest in Spiritualism, publishing a number of articles under the pseudonym of Arjuna (a prince from the Bhagavad Gita).

"In 1905, Madero became increasingly involved in opposition to the government of Porfirio Díaz. He organized political clubs and founded a political newspaper (El Demócrata) and a satirical periodical (El Mosco, "The Fly"). Madero's preferred candidate was again defeated by Porfirio Díaz's preferred candidate in the 1905 governmental elections.

"In a 1908 interview with U.S. journalist James Creelman published in Pearson's Magazine, Porfirio Díaz said that Mexico was ready for a democracy and that the 1910 presidential election would be a free election. Madero spent the bulk of 1908 writing a book at the directions of the spirits, which now included the spirit of Benito Juárez himself.

"The [resulting] book, published in late 1908, was titled La sucesión presidencial en 1910 (The Presidential Succession of 1910). The book quickly became a bestseller in Mexico. The book proclaimed that the concentration of absolute power in the hands of one man Porfirio Díaz for so long had made Mexico sick. Madero pointed out the irony that in 1871, Porfirio Díaz's political slogan had been "No Reelection". Madero acknowledged that Porfirio Díaz had brought peace and a measure of economic growth to Mexico.

"However, Madero argued that this was counterbalanced by the dramatic loss of freedom which included the brutal treatment of the Yaqui people, the repression of workers in Cananea, excessive concessions to the United States, and an unhealthy centralization of politics around the person of the president.

"Madero called for a return of the Liberal 1857 Constitution of Mexico. To achieve this, Madero proposed organizing a Democratic Party under the slogan Sufragio efectivo, no reelección ("Valid Suffrage, No Reelection"). Porfirio Díaz could either run in a free election or retire.

"Madero's book was well received, and many people began to call Madero the Apostle of Democracy. Madero sold off much of his property - often at a considerable loss - in order to finance anti- reelection activities throughout Mexico. He founded the Antir- eelection Center in Mexico City in May 1909, and soon thereafter lent his backing to the periodical El Antireeleccionista, which was run by the young lawyer/

philosopher José Vasconcelos. Madero traveled throughout Mexico giving antireelectionist speeches, and everywhere he went he was greeted by crowds of thousands.

'The Porfirian regime reacted by placing pressure on the Madero family's banking interests, and at one point even issued a warrant for Madero's arrest on the grounds of "unlawful transaction in rubber". Madero was not arrested, though, and in April 1910, the Antireelectionist Party met and selected Madero as their nominee for President of Mexico. Madero, worried that Porfirio Díaz would not willingly relinquish office, warned his supporters of the possibility of electoral fraud and proclaimed that "Force shall be met by force."

"Madero set out campaigning across the country and everywhere he was met by tens of thousands of cheering supporters. Finally, in June 1910, the Porfirian regime had him arrested in Monterrey and sent to a prison in San Luis Potosí. Approximately 5,000 other members of the Anti-Reelectionist movement were also jailed. Francisco Vázquez Gómez took over the nomination, but during Madero's time in jail, Díaz was "elected" as president with an electoral vote of 196 to 187.

"Madero's father used his influence with the state governor and posted a bond to gain Madero the right to move about the city on horseback during the day. On October 4, 1910, Madero galloped away from his guards and took refuge with sympathizers in a nearby village. He was then smuggled across the U.S. border, hidden in a baggage car by sympathetic railway workers.

"Madero set up shop in San Antonio, Texas, and quickly issued his Plan of San Luis Potosí, which had been written during his time in prison, partly with the help of Ramón López Velarde. The Plan proclaimed the elections of 1910 null and void, and called for an armed revolution to begin at 6 p.m. on November 20, 1910, against the illegitimate presidency/dictatorship of Díaz. At that point, Madero would declare himself provisional President of Mexico, and called for a general refusal to acknowledge the central government, restitution of land to villages and Indian communities, and freedom for political prisoners.

"On November 20, 1910, Madero arrived at the border and planned to meet up with 400 men raised by his uncle Catarino to launch an attack on Ciudad Porfirio Díaz (modern-day Pie- dras Negras, Coahuila). However, his uncle showed up late and brought only ten men.

"As such, Madero decided to postpone the revolution. Instead he and his brother Raúl (who had been given the same name as his late brother) traveled incognito to New Orleans, Louisiana.

"[Not until February 1911 did Madero enter] Mexico and led 130 men in an attack on Casas Grandes, Chihuahua. He spent the next several months as the head of the Mexican Revolution.

"Madero successfully imported arms from the United States, with the American government under William Howard Taft doing little to halt the flow of arms to the Mexican revolutionaries. By April, the Revolution had spread to eighteen states, including Morelos where the leader was Emiliano Zapata

"On April 1, 1911, Porfirio Díaz claimed that he had heard the voice of the people of Mexico, replaced his cabinet, and agreed to restitution of the lands of the dispossessed. Madero did not believe Díaz and instead demanded the resignation of President Díaz and Vice President Ramón Corral.

"Madero then attended a meeting with the other revolutionary leaders – they agreed to a fourteen-point plan which called for pay for revolutionary soldiers; the release of political prisoners; and the right of the revolutionaries to name several members of cabinet. Madero was moderate, however.

"He believed that the revolutionaries should proceed cautiously so as to minimize bloodshed and should strike a deal with Díaz if possible. In May, Madero wanted a ceasefire, but his fellow revolutionaries Pascual Orozco and Francisco Villa disagreed and went ahead with an attack on Ciudad Juárez.

"The revolutionaries won this battle decisively and on May 21, 1911, the Treaty of Ciudad Juárez was signed.

"Under the terms of the Treaty of Ciudad Juárez, Díaz and Corral agreed to resign by the end of May 1911, with Díaz's Minister of Foreign Affairs, Francisco León de la Barra, taking over as interim president solely for the purpose of calling general elections.

"This first phase of the Mexican [violent] Revolution thus ended with Díaz leaving for exile in Europe at the end of May 1911.

"On June 7, 1911, Madero entered Mexico City in triumph where [huge crowds shouted '¡Viva Madero!'....
"Before becoming president, Madero published another book, this one under the pseudonym of Bhima

(one of Arjuna's broth- ers in the Mahābhārata) called a Spiritualist Manual.

10. Chaotic Anti-Statist Political Revolution (1911-1916).
With Porfirio gone to Paris, chaotic Anti-Statism arose, President Madero soon found himself under siege by regional bosses who thought him to weak to lead Mexico and all sought to displace him. Madero selected General Victoriano Huerta to be his top general. Huerta used his position to put down most rebellions against the new government before arresting Madero to have him "shot while escaping prison." Huerta installed himself as President of Mexico (Feb. 13, 1913-Jul. 15, 1914)

For detailed accounts of this period, see the required reading:

Revolution in Mexico: Years of Upheaval, 1910-1940, by James W. Wilkie and Albert L. Michaels, especially pages 1-120 (noteworthy to understand the years 1913, 1914, 1915, 1916, 1917 are the articles by Lyle C. Brown, pages 60-72 and 112-115)

The problem of "Agrarian Reform" (really Land Tenure Reform) contributed to Madero's rise and fall. Several examples help us understand.

By 1911 Emiliano Zapata was destroying the sugar industry in the state of Morelos, directly south of Mexico City. He sought to end debt peonage on the sugar haciendas (rather than require fare wages and working conditions), and he set out to give the land to those who worked it (or let the peasants seize it), thus condemning the state of Morelos to long-term rural poverty for all. Zapata did not realize that where as the amount of land in finite, the growth of population is infinite.

zapata generated "faith" in land reform, favoring the land being returned to Ejidatarios as well as small and medium private farmers. Because Madero had called for Zapata to distribute land in a legal manner (with exact topographical measures, which seemed impossible given the extreme shortage of engineers), Marte R. Gómez, a young engineer, volunteered to join the newly formed Comisón Nacional Agraria.[30]

Marte R. Gómez tried to work with Zapata in his efforts at distributing land in 1915, but to conduct serious engineering in the crossfire of many battles between Zapata and the federal government, and between the zapatista factions themselves, was not possible. After months of problems in Morelos, Gómez moved in 1916 to work with the "radical' Governor of Yucatán Salvador Alvarado. With Avarado's departure, Gómez surveyed lands in the state of Campeche until 1921.

Rather then changing the conditions of workers held in debt peonage in Yucatán, General Salvador Alvarado (1915-1916) saw the solution as breaking up the henequen haciendas and distributing the land to the former debt peons. Those well-intended acts,

---

[30] Marte R. Gómez Oral History Interview with James Wilkie and Edna Monzón Wilkie, published in Wilkie and Wilkie, *Frente a la Revolución Mexicana: 17 Protagonistas de la Etapa Constructiva*, (México, D.F.: Universidad Autónoma Metropolitana), 4 volumes (Coordinating Editor: Rafael Rodríguez Castañeda): Vol 3. *Líderes: Salvador Abascal, Ramón Beteta, Marte R. Gómez, Jacinto B. Treviño* (2002).

however, helped bring the hacienda boom in Mexico to an end,[31] yet failed to break up many of the haciendas.

During this period many leaders believed that violent political action alone could achieve social and economic change, but in the end, most realized that achievement of political power was only the beginning of a long process to effect socio-economic change. In the meantime, Pancho Villa (from North Center Mexico fought Venustiano Carranza (from Northeast Mexico) and Alvaro Obregón (from Northwest Mexico). Carranza (joined by Obregón) defeated Villa by 1915-1916, and Carranza had Emiliano Zapata ambushed and killed in 1919.

11. Active-State Revolution (1917-1964) restored order by establishing the Constitution of 1917 to mediate between Statists in the government (backed by peasant and worker organizations) and Anti-Statists in the private sector. Carranza then convened the Constitutional Convention of 1916-1917 to write a new legal framework. Carranza signed the Constitution into law even thought he was unhappy with some of its provisions and never sought to enforce most of its provisions. In any case, enabling legislation had to be passed to implement the provisions and provide penalties for failure to do so and/or for violation of the provisions, this process being incremental and taking decades.

Oddly, the Constitution of 1917 was never ratified be the delegates who drafted it (and who in any case did not

---

[31] Other factors also intervened to end the henequen boom in Mexico. The advent of World War I cut into exports as did the cultivation of the plant around the world (Brazil, Madagascar, Tanzania, Manila), and the coming of synthetic rope and twine (especially nylon). Thus, the henequen industry began a long, slow decline (in spite of a mini-boom during World War II). See http://www.mexicomike.com/stories/henequen.htm

include the forces of Villa or Zapata). Nor was it approved by the state governments or voted on by the Mexican populace, much of which still lived in unpacified areas.

On the one hand, the Constitution reestablished the Crown's over arching policy by declaring that the State regulates all aspects of national life and economy, specifically adopting Santa Anna's decree of 1853 that and all land and sub-soil rights belong to the nation.

On the other hand, the Constitution of 1917 established a role for the private sector. The role has varied according to who has occupied the presidency. The President of Mexico has the sole power under the Constitution to decide whether or not to emphasize the role of the private sector at the expense of the government.

Thus the Constitution of 1917 is very important because it involved nationalizing mineral resources and prohibiting foreign businessmen from appealing to their home governments to protect their property.

Amended many times, the Constitution of 1917 remains in force, albeit with privatization of Ejidal land (1992) and mineral resources (1993)—except oil, gas, and electricity which remain under State ownership.

Unfortunately, however, the Constitution has prohibited re-election of all posts: federal, state, and local. Without re-election, experience is lost in short-term periods of office in the lower of house of Congress and mayoral level—three years in too little time to do anything and the wholesale turnover of positions means the first year is spent replacing staff, the second hoping they can learn what to do, and the third in closing the books.

Further, mayors are afraid to act because the fear that they will violate complex laws that cannot be quickly learned, and local government is usually too poor to fund a legal to offer guidance through the thicket of "normatividad" (normative) rules and regulations that seemingly block most mayoral actions.

Since 1934 Mexico's presidents serve six years, which has become too long as the pace of events has quickened in an era of ever-better communications. Four-year periods with re-election would now offer more effective government, but, alas, the memory of Porfirio Díaz's many re-elections live on. (Senators serve six years, as in the USA)

Five key Articles of the Constitution dominate Mexico to the present, especially as underlined below:

#3 requiring public education and that it be free and secular, the Church being prohibited from imparting primary education.

#27 reserving sub-soil rights to the State; protecting small and medium properties from land reform (but allowing the government to cap their size); requiring that haciendas be divided and returned to Ejidos (which Benito Juárez and Porfirio Díaz had sought to extinguish.

Article #27 required that the lands returned to the Ejidos and held by the community without the right to sell, rent, or use for collateral to obtain loans).

Further, Article #27 prohibited foreigners from owning land within 60 miles of the border and 30 miles from Mexico's coast as well as prohibited the Church from land ownership.

FOR FURTHER READING ON THE "TYPES OF [LAND] OWNERSHIP IN MEXICO,"

SEE:http://www.ricardobarraza.com typesofownershipinmexico.htm

#33 permitting Mexico's President on his sole order to deport forever any foreigner with no right to appeal;

#123 providing workers with: the right to strike, be paid for overtime work, be protected if injured or bearing children, be protected from employment if under age 12 and from night work if under 16.

#123 requires employers to indemnify workers who lose their jobs—one month pay for each year of work. Sindicatos (Labor Unions) were legalized and authorized to engage in collective bargaining with their employers and managers.

#130 authorizing the State to assume ownership of all Church properties, including those used for religious ceremonies; to prohibit Church oaths (thus outlawing monasteries); to authorize the states to regulate the number of clergy permitted to practice the "religious profession"; and, to prevent the clergy from voting, assembling for political purpose, criticizing the Constitution, or celebrating public activities or ceremonies.

The premise of the "Active State" is that it stands between Extreme Anti- Statism (too often leading to anarchism), and Extreme Statism (which leads to dictatorship).

The Active State anywhere yields to the private sector in business and industry in order to dedicate government activities to provide efficiently:

1. the traditional governmental services (e.g., police and fire protection, garbage collection, postal and telegraph systems, etc.),
2. public infrastructure (roads, railroads, electrical and water systems, telephone systems, etc.), and
3. social essential services (e.g., the construction and operation of public schools, clinics, hospitals, orphanages and social welfare programs for the poor, unwed mothers, and the aged).

Thus, in 1917 the State moves from a passive role to an active one as it seeks to solve problems not resolved by the private sector; and thus it subsidizes and/or invests in new and needed industry, often by providing high tariff protection.

To make the Active State function, Emilio Portes-Gil establishes in 1929 the "Official Party" (which has three names, as discussed below); but gradually it became more authoritarian during the 1960s, culminating in the murder of many hundreds (perhaps thousands) of persons who protested against it in the autumn of 1968 and during 1969. Thus, the Active State was converted to the "Statist Revolution" (1970-1982), discussed below.

Under Active State Revolution, the Central Government steadily acquired evermore power to "guide" national development. To end the chaos caused by roving rebel bands, it also deputized criminals as police, who agreed to limit their corruption. As under Porfirio Díaz, political and economic power was decentralized to rich regional elites, with the President serving as ultimate arbiter of disputes. The idea eventually came to encourage joint economic ventures linking domestic capital with foreign investment and technology.

11a. Political Phase (1917-1934), a new elite took power defeating scattered military rebellions to undertake the reconstruction of the country's economic infrastructure seriously damaged in the Revolution (that of 1910-1916, discussed above) and lead to the establishment of the Official Party in 1929, making explicit what had been implicit since 1921.

The Central Government rebuilt (often several times) the destruction caused by the Violent Phase of the Revolution (1911-1916, 1919) as well as military rebellions (1921-1923, 1927, 1929), established rural education in the early 1920s and the banking and finance system: Bank of Mexico in 1925 and the National Bank for Agricultural Credit in 1926—both under Manuel Gómez-Morín.

Presidents Alvaro Obregón (1920-1924) and Plutarco Elías-Calles (1924- 1928) led the activities to establish the Active State, with expanded roles for the Private Sector, still criticized by intellectuals and students for its excess of power under Díaz. Obregón successfully gained U.S. recognition of the Revolutionary Government.

In 1921, Obregón had conducted the first census since 1910. The census of 1921 showed the population to be 14.2 million, thus giving many journalists the idea that the demographic "cost" of violence in Mexico during those eleven years meant one million persons were killed since the population census of 1910.

But demographic historians do not equate "loss" with "killed." The calculation of Mexico's population calculated in Figure 2.

How Many Were Killed or "Lost" in the Violent Phase of the Mexican Revolution?

(Persons "Killed" After Adjusting for those "Lost" in Mexico's Upheaval, 1910-1921)

Population
  15.2 million in 1910
  -14.3 million in 1921
  = .9 million (900,000 apparently "killed")
  + .1 million (100,000) who fled from Mexico to personal security in the USA

  + .6 million (600,000) children not born owing to the fact that would be parents were at war and amid battles and insecurity--including the "soldadera" fighting with her man. (Armies moved with women involved in actual fighting and/or cooking and caring for their men and their encampments)

  + .1 million (100,000) not counted in the census, which was conducted with severe limitations. The year 1921 marked only the beginning of attempts to stabilize the country and rebuild the communications system that had been greatly damaged. Census-takers were unwilling (as were teachers and physicians) to go into much of rural Mexico, which was still a dangerous place. Further, Indigenous peoples in the jungles of Chiapas, for example, simply lived outside of "Mexico"— they knew only the name of their place or region, not the name of the country, about which many had never even heard about.

  = 1 million (100,000) Total "real" maximum "killed" in military action.

SOURCE: Adapted from data developed by Robert G. Greer.

This estimation of the number killed was calculated by Robert G. Greer, who made a new analysis of the data in 1966. Greer found that he could count the number of persons killed by military action during the decade after 1910 as only ranging from 75,000 to 100,000. [32]

Understanding how we get the "real" number of deaths by military action has always been too much for most observers to handle. And journalists wanted a high number to give a poetic ring to the magnitude of change wrought by the upheaval of Mexico between 1910 and 1921. Thus, the public mind has come to wrongly define the number "one million loss as one million killed.

Myth in this case of "deaths in battle" is more important than the "vague reality" of Mexico's eleven years of upheaval, in which between 75,000 and 100,000 may have been killed. (Tragically, many persons had always died in Mexico from causes other than military action: starvation, unavailability of medical treatment, interpersonal enmity, domestic violence, etc.)

The above myth about the "cost" to Mexico in numbers killed was important for Official Party of the Revolution to justify holding on to power "permanently", which ended in 2000.

Although it is a truism that "nothing is ever really permanent", we need to add a corollary: "except myth", which in this case of one million persons killed lives on.

From 1924 through 1934, the Private Sector dominated the "Continuing Revolution", which was led by Plutarco Elías Calles

---

[32] See Robert G. Greer, '"The Demographic Impact of the Mexican Revolution, 1910— 1921" (Austin, M.A. Thesis in Sociology, 1966), discussed by James Wilkie in *Statistics and National Policy* (Los Angeles: UCLA Latin American Center Publications, 1974). For nine views on the demographic impact after 1910 (including the view of Greer), see analysis by Robert MaCaa, *Missing millions: the human cost of the Mexican Revolution*, e-article, 2001, www.hist.umn.edu/~rmccaa/missmill/mxrev.htm

(who usually used his mother's last name "Calles," not his father's last name "Elías"). Although he was known as "El Jefe Máximo" and favored Ejidos run by individual families, the government was poor in relation to the Private Sector, which was able to operate with little regulation.

With regard to the Church, Calles was mistakenly quoted by a news reporter (who put words in Calles's mouth to get a sensational story), and those words seemingly threatened to implement provisions of the Constitution that had lain dormant. Lay (non-clerical) Catholics (encouraged by much of the clergy) rebelled in the Cristero War (1926-1929). They fought (1) against increasing state power limiting the Church's de facto "ownership" of buildings and land (and for private sector land rights in the face of government redistribution of land titles; and they fought (2) to maintain the Church's defacto control of primary education (which unconstitutional) of the country's children—both sides spoke more in terms of indoctrination than education.

When President-Elect Obregón was assassinated before he could retake office in 1928, Calles left for Europe to avoid the appearance of trying to retain power as the Strong Man of Mexico, which he eventually did become. In the meantime, Calles did not want to appear to be involved in the assassination—he and Obregón were supposed to have taken turns, but Obregón was killed by a Catholic priest before he could take office for his second term. (Father Miguel Pro did not know that a secret agreement had been reached between Church and State to end the Cristero War, and, arguing that under Catholic doctrine the Church had the moral right to "execute" its enemies, he took it upon himself to shoot Obregón at an open-air lunch, thus setting back the secret accord.)

While Calles was in Europe, however, Interim President Emilio Portes-Gil served during a 14-month interlude (1928-1930) to change the landscape of Mexico by undertaking rapid land distribution (which he knew that Calles opposed), Portes and he did so with the help of Marte R. Gómez—his

Secretary of Agriculture, with whom he worked to distribute land in Tamaulipas. (Portes Gil had been Governor of Tamaulipas, 1925-1928).

Portes did more in his 14 months than any President in Mexico's history, for example by

i. establishing University autonomy,
ii. developing the country's first real labor law (that Calles opposed),
iii. putting down a brief military rebellion led by General José Gonzalo-Escobar (who was supported by one-third of the officer corps and 30,000 troops and who were thought to be trying to link up with the Cristeros),
iv. signing the accord with the Archbishop of Mexico to end the Cristero War—the Church feared that unless it reinstated the mass, baptisms, marriages, and burial services (suspended in 1926 to force an uprising or protest against the government) feared that its power of the masses would be lost because there had been no real protest and the Catholic rites seemed to be headed into oblivion in Mexico,
v. founding the Official Party as the PNR (which many joked meant "Plutarco Necesita Robar"—contributing to a dramatic misundertanding of the PRN's role that removed Calles to indirect oversite of the Mexican government),
vi. holding a new presidential election to replace the assassinated Obregón.

For the presidential "election" of 1929 Calles proved how out of touch he was in Europe. He had believed, when he brought Pascual Ortiz-Rubio (an engineer and diplomat) from his post as Mexican

Ambassador to Brazil to become President of Mexico, that this act would neutralize the internal political struggles that threatened his planned role as Mexico's "Strong Man" when he returned from Europe in 1930. However, this man Calles had selected to "win" the presidency in 1929 was not the puppet president for whom he had hoped.

Ortiz Rubio not only refused to follow Calles' orders but believed that he could govern in his own right—even though he was in a weak leader with no real political support in Mexico. Back in Mexico, Calles saw Ortiz Rubio as being so ineffective that he was discrediting the concept of Calles being Mexico's Strong Man.

Hence in 1932, the trough of the world depression after 1929, Calles removed Ortiz-Rubio and placed into power General Abelardo Rodríguez, who as governor of Baja California had turned it into an attraction for American tourists seeking gambling and prostitution.

Ortiz Rubio and Rodríguez (as well as Portes Gil) had to cope with the arrival from the USA of nearly 500,000 Mexican workers who were "repatriated" to Mexico, forcibly or "voluntarily" to escape harassment, during the world depression.[33]

Whereas Portes-Gil had become President of Mexico as an independent force to negotiate the prevention of violence as Calles left the country during the investigation of the assassination of Obregón, Ortiz Rubio and Rodríguez won their jobs by being selected by the "dedazo"—the virtual "pointing of the finger" by Calles. Thus Ortiz Rubio and Rodríguez were "presidents" in name only.

---

[33] See *Journal of American History*, www.indiana.edu/~jah/mexico/mapstime.html

In contrast, Lázaro Cárdenas del Río (LC), who from 1936 through 1940 would be the President of Mexico, won his post with support from all regions of Mexico and was elected after he traveled to what seemed like every corner of the country (Calles was deported from Mexico by President Lázaro Cárdenas in 1936.)

The elite behind the Central Government constructed "One-Party Democracy" (PNR, 1929; PRM, 1938; PRI, 1946) under the "Official Party" (1929-2000). By the 1990s, this system was called the PRI-Gobi- erno (PRI Government), as the Official Party came to be known, making no distinction between the political party and the government.

Thus, the Official Party (which explicitly held the Presidency from 1929 through 2000) had three names:

Partido Nacional Revolucionario (PNR), 1929-1938;
Partido de la Revolucion Mexicana (PRM) 1938-1946;
Partido Revolucionario Institucional (PRI), 1946-2000,[34]

The PNR gave power to Mexico's regional bosses—the state governors and generals who controlled the military regions. The PNR articulated the realities of the 1920s, in which the state fought over such matters as

(a)whether land reform should create communally-owned farms (Eji- dos) as units for individual plots or (b) Ejidos worked collectively for farming and ranching.

Ejidos are not necessarily communal farms per se, but belong to the community, which authorizes how the land will be used,

---

[34] Since December 2000, the PRI is the "Former Official Party" (PRI/FOP), which still holds the sgovernorship of more than half of Mexico's state governments.

either by individual families working alone or groups of families working together in "communal" form. During the 1930s some thought that the idea of communes in the USSR were the same as communally run farms in Mexico, but there is no connection. The communes in the USSR had become, explicitly or implicitly, state farms under government ownership and control, which was not the case in Mexico.

Collective Ejidos should not be confused with Cooperatives made famous in the Wisconsin Dairy Belt of the USA by individual producers who maintain their independence except in the (1) collective bulk purchase of supplies and (2) marketing of the products. Collective negotiation for the purchase of supplies and sale of products has given the American Coops greater income.

As governor of the state of Michoacán (1928-1932), Lázaro Cárdenas del Río (LC) established his credentials as a "reformer" by implementing a) organization of new Sindicatos (Labor Unionism) [35]outside the control of Calles' corrupt Union leader Luis Morones;

---

[35] Sindicatos are the basis of Syndicalism, a type of economic system proposed as replacement for capitalism and state capitalism (sometimes called State socialism). Syndicalism utilizes federations of collectivist Sindicatos to achieve political goals   as well as economic goals. For adherents, Sindicatos are the potential means of both overcoming capitalist exploitation of the workers and running society fairly in the interest of the majority. Industry in a Syndicalist system theoretically is administer through cooperative alliances and mutual aid. Local Syndicates communicate with other Syndicatos through their Sector in a political party—in Mexico the Official Party. (In 1923, e.g., Diego Rivera founded the Sindicato de Obreros Técnicos, Pintores, Escultores y Grabadores Revolucionarios de México.) "An emphasis on industrial organization was a distinguishing feature of syndicalism when it began to be identified as a distinct current at the beginning of the 20th century…, seeing trade unions as simply a stepping stone to common ownership." (Adapted from http://en.wikipedia. org/wiki/Syndicalism and http://www.answers.com/topic/syndicalism)

(b) a new school curriculum involving the teaching of socialist and sexual education; and (c) the distribution of lands to Ejidatarios.

When Calles ordered from Europe that President Portes-Gil and Gov. Cardenas cease such distributions they both refused. The Governor openly ignored Calles' order, and seemingly sealed his fate—he would not receive Calles' dedazo to become Mexico's President for the period from 1934 to 1940.

Nevertheless, the depth of the world depression and its impact upon Mexico soon made Calles realize that Mexico needed a reform governor in power who could be compared to the executive role that FDR had enjoyed in the state of New York (1929-1932) before he became the U.S. President in 1933.

11b. Social Phase (1934-1940)

Lázaro Cárdenas (LC), President for this newly established six-year term (beginning December 1, 1934 and ending December 1, 1940) set out to give Ejidatarios and factory workers real power (built upon the accomplishments of Portes Gil, 1928-1930) to undertake full "land reform". LC distributed more good land than anyone before or after. To help foster agricultural development by Ejidatarios (who had no collateral because until they did not have title to their land until the 1990s), he founded the Bank for Ejido Credit—the Bank of Agricultural Credit (1926) had turned out to be focused on private credit based on the collateral of the title to their property.

> [FLASH FORWARD: Subsequently the Ejidal Bank would have to cancel all unpaid loans because most Ejidatarios were too poor to repay or had suffered bad-crop years (extreme weather, pests, lack of fertilizers). Those who had not paid could not borrow unless their debts were periodically cancelled. Ejidatarios soon learned that if

they did not pay, their debts would be wiped out and they could get a fresh start—certainly not an incentive to ever repay loans.)

Before LC could act with a free hand, in 1936 he had to deport from Mexico Calles and his openly corrupt cronies Luis Morones and Melchor Ortega, who opposed strikes and land reform backed by LC. This deportation was carried out smoothly, thus ending the strikes that had paralyzed the country to support Cárdenas against Calles. LC did this by recognizing Vicente Lombardo-Toledano as Supreme Leader of all Sindicatos (Labor Unions with political goal as well as economic goals), taking power from the grasp of Morones and Ortega, who had favored private factory owners since they headed the labor movement under Calles (1924-1928, 1931-1935).

Taking the government into directly controlling agricultural production and consumption, Cárdenas established in 1937 (CEIMSA) the agency that would become officially known in 1961 as CONASUPO. CONASUPO was subsidized by the government from 1937 through 1999 to pay fair prices to farmers and charge low prices to consumers for basic foods. In 1935, Cárdenas had established ANDSA, National Silos and Depositories for Seeds and Grains, to prevent private dealers from buying critical supplies at low prices during the harvest season and hoarding them until winter shortages drive up the prices. In 1939 Cárdenas established Father, in 1939 he established the agency that would known as DICONSA to distribute food supplies and open stores throughout all Mexico.

When Lázaro left office in December 1940, he declared that, with 42% of the agriculturally employed population having received land (13% of Mexico's land surface having been distributed since 1917), that the land reform had been completed, little knowing that he had only set the bar for the Official Party about how to use further land distribution as the test of "revolutionaryness."

In 1938, Cárdenas nationalized the foreign-owned petroleum industry and created PEMEx as the state oil company created to administer and improve the "hated" expropriated petroleum companies. LC left the PEMEx Labor Union in charge of newly nationalized industry. Subsequently all politics about PEMEx has revolved around how to implement increasingly greater control of professional petroleum engineers who have a world view if matters rather than worker control for their own interests. The idea that "PEMEx belongs to the Mexican people is ludicrous"—it belongs to the entrenched workers, whose union benefits from "sweetheart" contracts and ability to overrule rationale professional decisions, thereby making professional management subservient to the PEMEx Union which should only be "co-equal."

The theory of such nationalizations meant that profits could be generated for non-private use such as the building of schools, clinics, roads, scholarships, and higher worker salaries, while also generating reasonable taxes to be paid to the federal government. Unfortunately PEMEx soon acquired double the number of workers needed, many of whom were like Díaz's army and police—positions left vacant but still budgeted, thus leaving funds to be used corruptly. (Whereas Díaz had a phantom army of army and police, the PEMEx labor Union has a phantom army of workers.) Until the mid-1970s PEMEx lost huge amounts of money and had to be subsidized. (Because of "accounting" problems, PEMEx still is not sure what it costs to produce one barrel of oil.)

Lázaro Cárdenas was then free to complete nationalization of most of the country's railway system, creating Ferrocarriles Nacionales de México, which dealt a severe blow to the henequen industry in the Yucatán (as did Cárdenas seizure of many haciendas for redistribution to the workers on the henequen plantations) who no longer had easy transport from fields to port.

Most importantly, Lázaro Cárdenas secretly launched three major "economic revolutions," the first announced with little fanfare so as not to disappoint his leftist base of support:

i. Industrial Revolution in Mexico (1934—) that arose by inking the Government to the Private Sector (except PEMEx). To accomplish this task, he created the National Development Bank (NAFINSA) in 1934.[36]
NAFINSA's second epoch began under President Manuel Avila- Camacho in 1941, who expanded its investment in industry and infrastructure (e.g., transportation, subsidy of private companies), Avila-Camacho mistakenly has received all the credit for the industrialization boom fostered by Cárdenas.
ii. Green Revolutions in World Agricultural Productivity (1940—) that arose through the arranging the basis for establishing in Mexico the International Center for the Improvement of Corn and Wheat (CIMMyT).

---

[36] Según Wikipedia, LA PRIMERA ETAPA de The National Development Bank (NAFINSA) fue promovido en 1934 por el secretario de Hacienda Marte R. Gómez, que dio origen a Nacional Financiera.
Nacional Financiera es el cuarto paso que se da en el campo de la organización bancaria nacional. Se suma al Banco de México, al Banco Nacional de Crédito Agrícola y al Banco Nacional Hipotecario Urbano y de Obras Públicas, y operará como todas las instituciones aquí enumeradas para bien de la economía mexicana y para provecho de toda la Nación"
En esta etapa la labor de Nacional Financiera se enfocó, principalmente, a reincorporar a la economía privada los bienes inmuebles adjudicados al gobierno y a los antiguos bancos de emisión. Al mismo tiempo, de manera paulatina empezó a adquirir importancia como organismo de fomento del mercado de valores al emitir, en 1937, sus primeros títulos financieros e intervenir, en el mismo año, en la emisión de valores bancarios e industriales.

CIMMyT was developed when Professor Norman E. Borlaug arrived in Mexico as part of a team from the USA to establish the First Green Agricultural Revolution. Borlaug spent 20 years developing high-quality wheat that could thrive in Mexico's difficult conditions of fierce winds and problematic water supply as well as nutritionally depleted soils. Because Borlaug's new wheat seeds and grain came to fruition just in time him to organize Mexican exports to save India and Pakistan from famine in 1967.

"After India gained independence in 1947, the country couldn't even dream of feeding its population. Importing food wasn't possible because India lacked the cash to pay. India relied on food donated by the U.S. government.

En 1939 la institución logró elevados niveles en el otorgamiento de crédito y en la compraventa de valores, además de intervenir crecientemente en la emisión y colocación de acciones y bonos industriales.

Etapa Segunda "Promoción de la inversión productiva"

A principios de la década de 1940, el gobierno estableció el desarrollo de la infraestructura del país y la promoción de la inversión productiva como los objetivos esenciales de la labor de Nacional Financiera. See http://es.wikipedia.org/wiki/ Nacional_ Financiera_(México)#Etapa_Primera_.22Movilizaci.C3.B3n_del_ ahorro_ nacional.22 (March 23, 2010).

"In 1967, then-Prime Minister Indira Gandhi imported 18,000 tons of hybrid wheat seeds from Mexico. The effect was miraculous. The wheat harvest that year was so bountiful that grain overflowed storage facilities.

"Those seeds required chemical fertilizers to maximize yield. The challenge was to make fertilizers affordable to farmers who lacked the cash to pay for even the basics—food, clothing and shelter.

"Back then, giving cash or vouchers to millions of farmers living all over India seemed like an impossible task fraught with the potential for corruption. So the government paid subsidies to fertilizer companies, who agreed to sell for less than the cost of production, at prices set by the government.

"The subsidies were designed to make up the difference between the production price and sale price—and to give the producers a 12% after-tax return on any equity investment."[37]

FLASH FORWARD: This system in India was highly productive through the 1980s, but then failed, as is discussed in Section 13b, below.]

For this feat, Borlaug earned the Nobel Prize in 1970, and at the award ceremony in Stockholm, he acknowledged the research of his Mexican Research Team at CIMMyT.

The establishment of CIMMyT arrival in Mexico was possible only because Lázaro Cárdenas had asked Henry Wallace (U.S. Vice-President Elect and former U.S. Secretary of Agriculture) for help Mexico in resolving the failure of the Ejido system to produce food for its emerging urban sector.

Cárdenas named Marte R. Gómez as Secretary of Agriculture to assure national food supply during the difficult transition in December 1940 to the Presidency of Avila-Camacho.

---

[37] http://online.wsj.com/article/SB10001424052748703615904575052 9216127238 44.html?KEYWORDS=green+revolution+in+India

[FLASH FORWARD: Borlaug's Second Green Agricultural Revolution would not come until May 1999 (see Part 13b, below), when he announced in Mexico of having doubled the amount of protein in corn seeds.]

iii. Tourist Industry in Mexico (since 1940), being led by Gen. Juan Andreu Almazán as the inadvertent result of Lázaro NOT having chosen Almazán to be the Official Party candidate in 1940, as is discussed below.

Further, Lázaro Cárdenas transformed in 1938 the Official Party from the PNR (based on political bosses) into the PRM to based on "Corporativism", that is government based upon social sectors of related to occupation, in the style of Mussolini (who many Latin American economic ideologues in the 1920s and 1930s saw as having created economic stability in Italy).

Corporativism, which has continued up to this day to dominate the thinking of rank-and-file Sindicato members because their leaders "cogovern" with management. For example, in the case of the Secretariat of Education, government officials determine policy and textbooks, but the Teachers Union determines where teachers are assigned and which teachers are promoted.

To protect themselves politically and mobilize votes, artists joined Sindicatos, as the photo of Diego Rivera and Frida Kahlo suggests (see Figure 3). In my view, Corporativism (a politico economic system of state capitalism established by such dictators as Mussolini, Hitler, and Stalin in the 1920s and 1930s) should not be confused with "Corporatism"

FIGURE 3

Diego Rivera and Frida Kahlo

Diego Rivera and Frida Kahlo lead protest march by the Sindicato of Painters and Sculptors (This Sindicato was established by Rivera in 1923 and he was an active leader until his death in 1957.) The memory lives on and this photo has been a symbol for such movements as the protest against the Official Party in 1968 as can be seen in http://gatopardo. blogia.com/temas/informe-femospp-crimenes-de-la-guerra-sucia-en-mexico.php that is the basis of Western private capitalism[38] wherein Western private corporations the conformity of boosterism,[39] as in Sinclair Lewis's novel Babbit (1922).[40]

The Corporatist system involves the requirement that all large private enterprises (and some key medium-size private companies) join associations such as Chambers, such as the Chambers of Industry and Chambers of Commercial Activity. These associations (or Groups of Power) did not fit within the Official Party, but hold an advisory role with a direct line to the President of Mexico to represent the views of their member Private Companies as well as to negotiate benefits for Corporativist associations of workers represented by their Sindicatos. The Chambers, which represent private capital, were theoretically excluded from politics, but gained greater political importance than if they were in one of the four sectors of the Official Party (or since 2000 in any political party): This because of their direct access to Mexico's supreme political leader—the President.

The PRM set forth four sectors, which were supposed to select the Official Party's candidate to be President and generate policy, but in reality simply followed presidential orders:

1. Peasant Sector (organized as a consortium of Ligas de Campesinos under the name CNC—Confederación de Campesinos de México)

---

[38] Some sources do confuse the two terms and one can see the confusion caused by doing so in, for example: http://en.wikipedia.org/wiki/Corporatism

[39] See http://en.wikipedia.org/wiki/Boosterism

[40] http://en.wikipedia.org/wiki/Babbitt

2. Industrial Labor (organized as a consortium of Sindicatos as the CTM—Confederación de Trabajadores de México), founded and led since 1936 by Vicente Lombardo-Toledano (VLT)
3. Popular Sector (e.g., professionals, small/medium private business persons, bureaucratic Sindicatos)
4. Military Sector (organized by rank)

The most important Group in Mexico (the Group of bankers and industrialists) was left out of the PRM but given an advisory role to the President. This Group turned out to be much more important than the any of the four sectors of the Official Party.

With regard to the right of women to vote, "Lázaro Cárdenas drafted a bill to implement female suffrage, which was passed by both the Senate and Chamber of Deputies, was ratified by the states, and only needed formal declaration to be made into law. That declaration never came. The presence of a number of street demonstrations [for and against], a threatened hunger strikes by feminists, and fears that women would be unduly influenced by the clerical vote, unnerved Cárdenas at the last moment. Since the suffrage campaign was not a mass movement, it was easy to let the needed declaration slip away."[41]

Perhaps Lázaro recalled the scandal of his having offered sexual education during his governorship of the state of Michoacán and the failed attempt to do so during his presidency—in those cases public gossip claimed that he was attempting to prostitute women. Until the 1950s, many men and even some women saw the role of women as that of remaining outside the political sphere.

---

41 Quote is from www.womeninworldhistory.com/essay-06-04.html

President Lázaro Cárdenas showed his openness to a plural society:

i. He tried to protect Leon Trotsky, who was welcomed in 1937 after escaping
ii. from Stalin's secret agents, one of whom will murder him in Mexico City in 1940;
iii. Cárdenas met with Republican Spaniards who continue to arrive after having escaped from the Fascist "victory" in Spain by General Francisco Franco;
iv. Cárdenas increased government loans and subsidies to private industry even as he deepened the role of the Corporativist sindicatos to co-govern industry with the private owners;
v. Cárdenas and his Official Political Party-Government allowed (facilitated?) the registration of a new political party, the private- sector-based PAN (backed by the Church through its network of parish priests).

In 1939, Manuel Gómez-Morín founded the Partido Acción Nacional (PAN) to represent the private sector as well as the population that is oriented toward following the dictums of the Catholic Church (but not necessarily the priests). The PAN originally feared that Cárdenas was a Statist, but later came to realize that he was not.

> [FLASH FORWARD: Gaining force slowly but steadily, the PAN will not win its first governorship until 1988 in Baja California and its first Presidency of Mexico in 2000.[42]]

---

42 Gómez-Morín's oral history interviews are in *Frente a la Revolución Mexicana Frente a la Revolución* Mexicana: 17 Protagonistas de la Etapa Constructiva, by the Wilkies, Vol. 2 (2001), www.profmex.org/mexicoandtheworld/volume7/3summer02/02index3.htm

In the meantime, Gómez-Morín and the PAN faced opposition from among some lay Catholics who thought voting to be the useless voting but the Official Party did not really count the votes. Thus, in 1937 Salvador Abascal had established the Sinarquistas Movement to make its protest against the "Communist" government, and rather than trying to vote or to use the violence of the Cristeros, Abascal organized non-violent marches of peasants throughout West-Central Mexico. Sinarquismo (without anarchy) sought to remake Mexico on the model of Francisco Franco (which was emerging in the Spanish Civil War)—Franco based his government on an alliance with the Roman Catholic Church.

Discredited by 1941 as his followers tired of peacefully marching and marching without any results, Abascal left for Baja California where he established Colonia María Auxiliadora to prove his claim that, with God's help, he could make the dry dessert bloom with food. His colony there would completely fail in 1946; and he and his followers had to be saved, ironically by Lázaro Cárdenas, who after leaving the presidency in 1940 would serve as Mexico's Minister of Defense during World War II.

Meanwhile as President, Lázaro Cárdenas invested government funds in private companies to spur new industry. Even before he left office, he privately admitted the economic failure of most of the Ejido system. To smooth the transition to Avila-Camacho, who "won" the election of 1940,

Lázaro Cárdenas named Marte R. Gómez Secretary of Agriculture to span his government to that of MAC, and the U.S. Government sent to the inauguration Henry Wallace to assure all Mexico that, on the eve of World War II, the USA recognized the victory of the Official Party candidate, thus forestalling a military revolution led by the losing candidate.

The loser in the Presidential Election of 1940 was General Juan Andreu Almazán, who had built the roads of North-East Mexico and the Railroad from the "Mainland Mexico" to the Peninsula of Yucatán. (He was backed in his campaign for the presidency by Diego Rivera, who saw the LC and "his" Official Party as having become "Stalinist in control of State power.)

Almazán did not rise in arms with his troops when he lost the rigged election of 1940 (as had been the tradition for "strongmen"), but rather he "retired" to Acapulco to initiate the Mexican Tourist Industry. He realized that Acapulco was the future of tourism, especially attracting Hollywood types who could not go on vacation to Europe after World War II began. Having broken with the Official Party, however, Almazán was left out of the Official History of Mexico, in which President Miguel Alemán is the hero in the story of how the tourist industry was established.

In the meantime, Lázaro established the country's social security system, which would become IMSS (Instituto Mexicano de Seguro Social) under his successor. Avila-Camacho has mistakenly received all of the credit for the establishment of IMSS.

[CLARIFICATION: In Mexico, IMSS covers (i) retirement for most at age 65 and (ii) health without age limit for all contributing workers and their families. (In contrast, U.S. Medicare is separate from U.S. Social Security and both are limited because they only begin for most at age 65.) Worker disability is covered (poorly) in both countries after minimum period of work history.]

The population of Mexico grew from 16.6 million in 1930 to 19.7 million in 1940, this growth encourage by President Cárdenas because he saw Mexico as lacking the population to become consumers of Mexican industrial production. Indeed, Mexico's population did not reach its Pre-Colonial level of 25 million until 1950 (as shown in Booklet of Charts, Chart 3).

11c. Economic Phase (1940s-1950s

Presidents Manuel Avila-Camacho (MAC, 1940-1946) and Miguel Alemán (1946-1952) also oversaw the Mexico's Industrial Revolution and its "Economic Miracle" (1951-1980), which saw low inflation as well as high GDP growth (averaging 6.4% yearly) under Presidents Adolfo Ruiz-Cortines (1952-1958) and Adolfo López-Mateos (ALM, 1958-1964). shows restoration of economic growth stability that had been lost with the fall of Díaz.

To assure political stability, during World War II, MAC spearheaded the establishment of the Law of Social Dissolution in 1941. Initially this new Law was aimed against the "fascist" tendencies of the time, but it was not revoked until three decades later and was frequently used against leftists and other dissidents, who were, supposedly trying to "dissolve" society). In 1947 the strings on labor unions were tightened, as the Ministry of Labor was granted the right to refuse to accept the legitimacy of elected union officials—which, in fact, gave the Ministry the power to appoint "suitable" persons as union leaders instead of elected ones.[43]

Those who resisted the imposition of Official Party such dictums as the one that gave the government full control over the labor sector could be and were charged with violating the Law of Social Dissolution. Indeed this Law would prove to be useful to the Official Party during the Cold War, especially after Fidel Castro came to power in Cuba beginning January 1, 1959. The political situation in Mexico was "threatened" by events in Cuba, which became a counter-model to that of the PRI because comparison to Mexico was inevitable. On the one hand, one part of the Mexican government had helped Fidel launch his invasion of Cuba from Mexico in 1956, but on the other hand the question became "could the PRI be supplanted by a "hidden" Mexican "Communist"

---

43 See Pekka Valtonen, "Political Discourse, the State and the Private Sector in Mexico, 1940-1982" Artikkelit Lokakuu (2000)_www.helsinki.fi/hum/ibero/xaman/ articulos/2000_05/valtonen.html

Group? The Left in Mexico did claim that the Cuban model meant true Revolution compared to the PRI, which only administered "Mexico's dead Revolution." The leftist, nationalistic was at its apex.

The role of Communism in Mexico, the ideology of the protest movements taking place there from 1958 through 1968, and the difficult logic of Mexico's relationship with U.S.-Cuba relationship complicated the ideological and economic situation of Mexico, especially in light of the profoundly different views the two nations had of the Cold War.

"The Cold War world," writes Julia Sloan, "was governed by the bipolarity established and enforced by the United States and the Soviet Union. Within this context, the superpowers engaged in a global struggle for nothing less than 'the soul of mankind,' each advancing their own agendas for the betterment of all. The bipolarity consists in how the two powers did it: Russia, in a statist, and the U.S. in Anti-statist way.

But America's Anti-Statism and its Cold War Grand strategy studies in historical, and international perspective, was and is still based on suspicion of state power. Such anti-statis inclinations prevented anxieties from converting the United States into a garrison that it might possibly become in its absence. This trait of the American state served as a fountain of national strengths that allowed the U.S. to outperform its supremely centralized, statist rival, the USSR. Its principled belief in limiting federal power protected the economy and public support for Cold War activities, says Aaron Friedberg in "The Shadow Of The Garrison".

For the United States the route to progress lay in modernization through democratic capitalism, involving bringing the world's poorer nations into the international economy and elevating the living conditions of their people. Conversely the Soviet Union similarly advanced improvements in the material quality of life for the world's poor, but through the communist system. Thus, both super-powers had essentially the same broad agenda, but diametrically opposed ideologies governing how to achieve it.

"Practically, however, their methods for reaching this goal were not so far apart, both involving the assertion of their military and economic power over the world's weaker and poorer nations.

"Mexico was one such nation. For the United States the Cold War was a global struggle against communism as embodied by the totalitarian Soviet state. The United States government and a significant portion of its citizenry considered communism an evil force in the world, one that must be combated with all available ideological, military, and financial means. Mexicans, and Latin Americans in general, on the other hand took a much less critical view of communism and were less likely to associate all things communist with the Soviet Union. As a result, [Many] Mexicans viewed the Cold War not as a principled crusade, but as an example of aggression by [two] imperialist states whose financial and military power allowed them to dominate less developed countries.]"[44]

Indeed, for both the USA and USSR Mexico City became the international spy capital of the Americas to "listen" to each other's radio traffic covering military activities in the Americas and Cuba's military traffic about it intelligence and counter-intelligence. As the spy capital, Mexico City became the home in the Americas for governmental spies for every major country in the World, all seeking to spy upon each other as well as their county's "enemies".

> [FLASH FORWARD: Before Lee Harvey Oswald (a former U.S. military sharpshooter) assassinated President Kennedy in 1963, he visited the Russian Embassy in

---

44 See Julia Sloan, "Carnivalizing the Cold War," *European Journal of American Studies* (2009) http://ejas.revues.org/document7527.html

Mexico City. Oddly enough, by then Oswald had not only tried during a two-year stay in Russia to obtain citizenship there, but had threatened at the U.S. Consulate in Moscow to renounce his U.S. citizenship. Although Russia rejected his application to be a citizen, the question arises about his possible role as "double agent" or perhaps "triple agent" and for whom? (He lived in Russia from October 1959 to May 1962, employed for several years in Minsk at an electronics factory as a lathe operator, and also receiving a subsidy from the Soviet Red Cross)

U.S. intelligence was "officially" as confused about Oswald's visit to the Russian Embassy as they were when they sent the FBI to investigate American citizens for supposedly having openly (and legally) visited the Soviet Embassy in Mexico City—the FBI had informants at all universities in Mexico City and 24-hour film surveillance of "open visits", but because so many informants gave erroneous information to gain bonuses, the FBI never could be sure that if it had been able to film "all persons" who had supposedly "met with the Soviets." Ironically, at that time the FBI was operating illegally in Mexico (FBI worked in the USA, CIA outside USA), and when the U.S. Justice Department found out, the FBI had to depart from Mexico.]

PRI Presidents MAC, Alemán, and ARC before and during the Cold War authorized and encouraged the rise of joint U.S.-Mexican private companies, who were protected against nationalization by accepting a representative of the PRI as member of the private company's board, much to the consternation of many anti-American intellectuals in Mexico.

Mexico's Private Sector, however, used its privileged relationship to Mexico's Presidents in the country's Corporativism system, to gain an alliance with the State and its powerful Ministry of Gobernación from 1941 through 1970. In the latter year,

Meanwhile, President Avila-Camacho had authorized in 1942 the Mexico to cooperate with the U.S. Emergency Farm Labor Program (Bracero Program) allowing Mexicans to perform contract work in the United States for a fixed period. Over the next 22 years of the program's existence, more than 4.6 million labor contracts were officially issued with many workers traveling to the USA outside the U.S. law, which was laxly enforced. This eased internal pressures in Mexico, where the rural sector could not accommodate millions of workers on worn-out and eroded lands; and it sent workers to the USA instead of to Mexico City where by sheer numbers they would have driven down the industrial wage level.

In 1944 MAC established the State Company to Buy, Regulate, and Distribute Milk, which in 1964 would be renamed "Leche CONASUPO." The name was shortened to LICONSA in 1994 and continues in operation today, albeit with the State share of ownership falling from 100% to majority to at least 51% State owned. Because Mexico has had problems in producing enough milk, it has imported powered milk from abroad and reconstituted it with purified water to distribute in liquid form, selling at subsidized price.[45] Beginning in the 1940s, the State developed a complicated infrastructure to assist CONASUPO buying and distributing milk and food to the poor—some of it at very little or no price to alleviate poverty—especially in marginal urban and isolated rural areas.

MAC's Minister of Gobernación (Internal Political Control) was Miguel Alemán, who took office with the idea of expanding industrialization in Mexico.

---

45   See http://www.liconsa.gob.mx/

To establish the change of government, he reformed the Official Party in 1946 by removing the Military Sector, making it subservient to the President rather than one of the "pillars" of the Corporativist political system. He renamed as the PRI (Partido Revolucionario Institucional). The change of name from Partido de la Revolución Mexicana (PRM) to Partido Revolucionario Institucional (PRI) signified that "the political elite wanted to make it crystal clear that stability was the name of the game—so that even revolutions could be institutionalized, no matter the conceptual contradiction. The corporatist party structure, with its labor (CTM) and peasant (CNC) sections, was able to contain feelings of disappointment or dissatisfaction from erupting in any collective, mass-based ways, by giving each sector a sense that its specific needs were being heard and taken care of at least to an extent. Instances of open conflict did occur—like the peasant campaign of Rubén Jaramillo in Morelos in 1953 (he and his family was finally assassinated by the army in 1962) - but they did not escalate to the point of seriously shaking the power structures. For sure, it is to be admitted, the mission of the PRI could not have been so successful without a considerable mass support—which is, no doubt, also one of the explanations for the longevity of its grip of the power."[46]

At the same time, Alemán moved to appoint to government posts university-educated leaders who held a B.A. or B.S. degree (Licenciatura, which required a thesis)—thus bringing to power the new Grupo de los Licenciados" (Lawyers, the title being abbreviated as "Lic', and some engineers—Ingenieros—holding B.S. degrees) Thus, Lic. Alemán shifted away from the policies of presidents through Gen. Cárdenas and General Avila-Camacho.

Thus, the Lawyers (1946-1964) replaced the

---

[46] From Pekka Valtonen, www.helsinki.fi/hum/ibero/ xaman/articulos/2000_05/ valtonen.html

Generals (1911-1946) who had replaced Díaz's
Científicos (1884-1911) as the basis for leadership.

Alemán downplayed land reform to build dams and distribute water throughout Mexico. He knew that Mexico had little water for irrigating crops. Water flowing from the Mississippi River alone being greater than that of all Mexico's rivers combined. More than 75% of Mexico's territory is unsuitable for agriculture because of the poor soil and arid climate. Also, for Alemán the building of dams could generate much need electricity for the modernization of the country.

Under Alemán's economic scheme of investment, TELMEx was founded in 1947 when a group of government-protected Mexican investors bought Swedish Ericsson's Mexican branch. In 1950 the same investors bought the Mexican branch of the ITT Corporation thus becoming the only telephone provider in the country—a private monopoly.[47]

Unfortunately TELMEx service virtually collapsed, and it became impossible to obtain or repair a telephone without bribing TELMEx employees. Even with a phone, to obtain a connection and then one to the correct number could take up to one hour. To change service from one person to another at the same address would necessitate cutting off service and waiting for up to five years, hence occupants at addresses changed but the phone remained under the original owner's name, rendering telephone directories totally useless.

To establish a State-owned industry to produce trucks at "reasonable cost," Alemán founded Diesel Nacional (DINA).

---

[47] See http://en.wikipedia.org/wiki/TELMEx

By 1963 President López Mateos would oversee an expansion of DINA to assemble buses in Mexico for Renault, later assembling and distributing autos for Renault as well. By 1980, President López Portillo would oversee DINA manufacturing and/or assembling15,000 trucks a year. But by this time, bureaucratic costs and inefficiencies would be completely unreasonable. [48]

In the meantime, in 1949 a new facet of the Green Revolution would get underway to improve Mexico's basic food—the tortilla. Roberto González-Barrera founded MASECA to manufacture tortilla flower with vitamins and mineral for shipment to the far regions of Mexico where its long-shelf life permitted him to help reduce the grueling problem faced by women: grinding and processing corn to make tortillas the hard way—with human own sweat. Too, González Barrera was successful in towns and cities where "fresh" tortilla dough was (and is) made in unhy- gienic conditions with filthy tap water and inefficient primitive equipment. Not only did (and does) that "fresh method" use excess water and electricity but the waste damages sewer systems.

The Alemán government was concerned that a private entrepreneur such as González-Barrera could enjoy success without making an alliance with the Official Party. (Most private corporations could not succeed without placing representatives of the Mexican government on their Board of Directors. The Directors guaranteed that the company would not be nationalized as long as it gave financial support to the Official Party and a fat fee to the government directors.

In an attempt to break MASECA, now part of Grupo MASECA (GRUMA), the government subsidized the establishment in 1952 of a "private" company—MINSA. A year later MINSA became fully

---

[48] See www.fundinguniverse.com/company-histories/Consorcio-G-Grupo-Dina-SA- de-CV-Company-History.html

state-owned under the name MICONSA to sell processed tortilla flower at fully subsidized prices, but fortunately for González-Barrera, like most bureaucrats they did not know (or care) about how to run a business; further they were years behind MASECA in technology. (In 1993 this money losing, inefficient operation was privatized by President Salinas, and by 2002 it would become a publicly traded corporation. In 2008 and 2009 it will try to catch up with GRUMA's low carbohydrate tortillas by offering its own high-fiber, corntortilla flower to reduce the high carbohydrate count in traditional low-fiber corn.)

With regard to the rights of women to vote and be voted for, Alemán granted those rights for local elections in 1947, but not to Indigenous women who continue to this day to fall under their village's "usos y costumbres." (Usos y costumbres are Indigenous "Laws" in which men own women and in which only men can vote. Ultimate decisions are made by the Council of Elders, who make decisions while intoxicated with alcohol—See Juan the Chamula by Ricardo Pozas, UC Press, 1962).

Ruiz Cortines gave women federal voting rights (and right to run for office) in 1953, effective only at the next federal election for the national Congress—1955.

11d. "Balanced" Phase (1958-1964). In what was hoped to be a transition from a closed PRI control of society, Adolfo López Mateos (ALM) was selected as the first PRI president to rise from a Ministry other than the Ministries of Defense or Gobernación (Internal Security). He rose from the Ministry of Labor. "to give workers attention that had been lost during the Mexico's Industrial Revolution" (see 11c, above), seeking to provide a balance that had been lacking in the Political, Social, and Economic Phases (11a, 11b, 11c) above.

ALM established his own idea of what the Active State should seek, but his rhetoric in favor of laborers inadvertently seemed to authorize in 1958-1960 general strikes by railway-electrical-telephone workers as well as telegraphers, teachers, and industrial workers. The broke out during the interim between ALM's election and taking office, complicating the change in power and weakening the ability of ALM to help workers because the PRI bureaucracy under his Minister of Gobernación was Gustavo Díaz-Ordaz (the evil enforcer of PRI discipline), who used harsh force to "restore order" (labor unionists would follow PRI orders through their Sindicato or face beatings and jail for having caused "Social Dissolution").

The strikes against the PRI set of an internal debate about how to react, and that gave important power to ALM's harsh Minister of Gobernación (hence the heir apparent to the Presidency), and ALM found that his velvet glove that he had wanted to extend had to be withdrawn in favor of the steel glove extended by his Minister Gustavo Díaz-Ordaz (GDO).

Disappointed by the turn of events, Carlos Fuentes articulated the intellectual view that the Revolution ended in 1959—his Death of Artemio Cruz is, in my view, the best novel written about Mexican history, rich in its understanding of issues in the "Many Mexicos."

To overcome his use of force against labor, ALM claimed to represent the "left" within the Revolution and maintained close relations with Fidel Castro's "One-Party-Revolution" in Cuba beginning in 1959. The PRI benefited from being "pro-guerilla" abroad but "anti-guerilla at home." Mexico always kept its Revolutionary credentials by providing a lifeline to Cuba against the U.S. blockade. ALM balanced this tilt to the left by inviting world leaders to Mexico, including Presidents John F. Kennedy and Charles de Gaulle.

In the meantime, Mexico continued to be the Cold War Listening Posts in the Western Hemisphere, spies flocking to Mexico City from every intelligence service in the world to keep tabs on the USA and Cuba and the relations of both with Mexico and all Latin America. The U.S. government was not pleased with ALM's refusal to break diplomatic relations with Cuba—the only country in the hemisphere not to break relations and seal of inexpensive trans-shipment of goods in and out of Cuba.

U.S. displeasure with ALM's stance regarding Cuba helped his wing of the PRI to claim that Mexican Revolution still burned brightly, thus masking ALM's further attacks on organized labor.

López Mateos burnished his Statist credentials by "nationalizing" in 1960 the foreign-owned electrical companies (which were pleased to be paid richly to leave Mexico quietly). ALM claimed that only the government could do what the private companies had not done —extend the grid of electricity to isolated rural areas. (In 1960 only 44% of Mexico's population had electricity.[49])

Ironically, this plan worked out only in part and resulted in the rise of a new government State-owned agency (The Mexican National Electrical Industry, especially Luz y Fuerza del Centro), which to this day is so highly corrupt and inefficient that it requires extensive subsidies from the central government, not to mention employing many thousands of fake "consultants" and "workers" (called "aviadores"—members of the "Mexican Royal Air Force"[50]

---

[49] A joke in Mexico at the time played upon ALM's words upon nationalization: "'The electricity now belongs to Mexico and its people'—too bad electricity has been cut by half a day and we never know which half ." With time, most power outages declined as did power surges that burn out equipment. Cf. http://www.cfe.gob.mx/en/LaEmpresa/ queescfe/historia/

[50]who fly into all government offices to collect their salary and who show up only on the payroll—not the job. (The corruption in the Sindicato Mexicano de Electricistas (SME)—involving the sale of electricity by SME to benefit the Sindicato behind the government's back—will not be addressed until 2009, as we will see below.)

ALM greatly expanded the role of the State by taxing TELMEx long- distance calls in order to order to generate a pool of funds to modernize switching equipment and lines throughout Mexico. [51]Thus, TELMEx operated as a private enterprise that cooperated with the Mexican government to deliver phone services to the nation, to a much more important extent than had been the case since 1950. TELMEx was under fire for its backlog in installing telephone service to business and homes—many years to wait, if no bribe paid to TELMEx union workers allied with the PRI. TELMEx operated as a private enterprise that cooperated with the Mexican government, both claiming falsely to be delivering improved phone services to the nation.

Further, ALM declared the petrochemical and mining industries to be of strategic importance to the Mexican government control.

With regard to the petrochemical industry,[52] in 1959 ALM established its development as a priority. He allowed the possibility of using private capital to develop the industry because the government had neither the expertise nor funds to do so. Although the petroleum industry as a whole is exclusively controlled by the

---

[50]   There is, of course, no "Royal Air Force in Mexico."

[51]   See www.fundinguniverse.com/company-histories/Telefonos-de-Mexico-SA-de-CV- Company-History.html

[52]   This discussion draws upon Alejandro López-Velarde, http://www.lvwa.com.mx/ doc3.pdf

State, in practice, private companies acquire the national products of the first processes from PEMEx or from abroad and with them create hundreds of chemicals which are transformed into articles for daily use. Under ALM the petrochemical industry developed greatly and production in the volume of petrochemicals increased 53 times, (359 petrochemical permits would be awarded between the years of 1961 and 1983, 163 of which were delivered to companies, and investment poured into Mexico.)

With regard to mining,[53] in 1961 ALM changed Mexican law to require that no more than 49% of investment in industry could be foreign, but in strategic industries such as coal mining foreign capital could not exceed 34%. All new investment had to be approved by the Mexican government, with bureaucratic delays running up to several years and/or being put on permanent hold so as not to say "no."[54]

> FLASH FORWARD: President Salinas will break this bottle-neck after 1989 when he decrees that the government answer to foreign petitions to invest in Mexico is automatically "yes"—if the government does not say "no" within 30 working days after receiving all petitions.

In the realm of cultural control by the State, ALM created the National Commission for Free Text Books, giving the PRI a vehicle to make pro- paganda in the primary schools—this at no cost to families of the students so accepted by most of the population who resented having to pay for privately printed textbooks. The

---

[53] On mining law in Mexico, see: www.bakernet.com/ NR/rdonlyres/9D4AA2AF- D856-4ECC-828A-D306D05A2564/40322/MiningLawinMexBro1.pdf

[54] See, e.g., the 1962 secret memo by the U.S. Embassy in Mexico City (which sought to understand ALM's "zigs" left, right, and back again: www.gwu.edu/~nsarchiv/ NSAEBB/NSAEBB124/doc25.pdf

textbooks were written by teachers trained in the Lázaro Cárdenas presidential era to spread the word about the evils of capitalism—much to the consternation of LC himself who saw the world in much more complicated terms and even invested government funds in private industry—albeit in a manner that was not publicly announced.

The film industry had already become involved in the struggle between the private sector and the State, and this intensified under ALM.[55] Whereas in 1947 President Alemán had converted the Banco Nacional Cinomatográfica (National Film Bank) into one based on government and union control as well as private capital with the goal of extolling the virtues of capitalism, ALM shifted to control of production from the private sector to the Sindicatos, including producers, directors, and writers as well as technical staff. These Sindicato members closed the door to innovation as well as to new people, hence unavoidably causing decline in quality (the writers union had to approve each new script as did the technical staffs). The resulting obvious decline in quality brought to an end Mexico's "Golden Age of Cinema" (1940s and 1950s). The decline of Mexican films in the 1960s was exacerbated by Hollywood's drive to recapture Mexican and Latin American film markets lost during World War II (when U.S. films focused on portraying the evils of Japan, Germany, and Italy). And the advent of television accessible to the masses in the 1950s began to siphon audiences out of the film theater monopoly of William O. Jenkins, who did not well maintain the Mexican theaters now full of the poorer classes for whom he was demanding grade B- and C+ films. State-run

---

55 This analysis draws upon Eduardo de la Vega Alfaro, "The Decline [and End] of the Golden age of Cinema...," in Joanne Hershfield and David R. Maciel, eds., *Mexico's Cinema: A Century of Film and Filmmakers* (Wilmington: Scholarly Resources, 1999) and www.drclas.harvard.edu/revista/articles/view/87

production of films would eventually become State-owned film production in the 1970s.

In the countryside, López Mateos reversed the decline in distribution of Ejido lands that had been the policy Avila Camacho, Alemán, and Ruiz- Cortines, reaching again almost the same level of agriculturally employed workers who were incorporated into Ejidos (41%) by LC. When ALM left office, the cumulative amount of land surface that had been distributed reached 27 (including the cumulative amount of 13% at the time when LC left office).

To facilitate the development and distribution of seeds, in 1960 ALM established PRONASE (the National Seed Producing Company).[56] This company along with CONASUPO worked well until they were later overwhelmed by the ever-expanding size and scope of activity throughout the country.

Hence food processors would begin to import quality grains by the 1970s, 1980s, and 1990s. The relatively reliable CONASUPO and PRONASE operations that Cárdenas and López Mateos established would fade with the rise of Statism after 1970.

ALM also nationalized the henequen industry on the Yucatán peninsula in 1964 to "save" that declining industry. He reorganized the industry as CORDEMEx,[57] but annual output declined from 131,267 metric tons in 1964 to 44,000 in 1990, when it was privatized by Salinas to stem further government financial losses and corruption.

---

[56] On PRONASE, see www.engormix.com/s_news_view.asp?news=2284&AREA=BAL

[57] See, e.g., http://findarticles.com/p/articles/mi_hb288/is_199103/ai_hibm1G141945330 and http://wwwmexicomike.com/stories/henequen.htm

For the U.S. Border with Mexico, ALM began the planning of the maquila industry, or plants free of Mexican import taxes if the processed goods are exported (taxes being only paid on value added such as wages to workers).58[58] With the U.S. termination by the Bracero Program in 1964, ALM realized that new employment would have to be found for the more than 50,000 workers waiting on the Mexican side of the border to work in the USA. ALM sent delegations study the Asia models and the groundwork was laid for the Border Industrialization Program to be officially launched in 1965 by President Diaz-Ordaz.

"Maquiladora" is primarily used to refer to factories in Mexican towns along the U.S.-Mexico border but increasingly is used to refer to factories all over Latin America. Maquiladora factories encompass a variety of industries including electronics, transportation, textile, and machinery, among others. Maquiladoras may be 100% foreign-owned (usually by U.S. companies) in most countries. The use of Maquiladoras is an example of off shoring. Other countries such as Hong Kong, Singapore, Taiwan, South Korea, Japan, and German have Maquiladoras as well, but the majority of them are located in Mexico and are associated with companies from any country mainly seeking access to the U.S. markets. (The term "maquiladora", in the Spanish language, refers to the practice of millers charging a "maquila", or "miller's portion" for processing other people's grain.)

Mexico's population grew from 25 million in 1950 to 41 million in 1964.

12 State Capitalism and "Dirty War" (1965-1982) Under 3 Presidents, who order the murder (with plausible deniability) of many of the PRI's opponents.

---

58 See, e.g.: http://www.medc.org/roots_maquila.php, http://tripatlas. com/Maquiladora, and http://www.jstor.org/pss/20080194

This is the era of the "Dirty Three Presidents":
Gustavo Díaz Ordaz (GDO), 1964-1970
Luis Echeverría Álvarez (LEA), 1970-1976, and
José López Portillo (JOLOPO), 1976-1982

Although these three presidents were "lawyers", they took power as the generation of arrogant "No-Nothings" Thug, [59]who replaced the Generation of Lawyers (1946-1964) that had replaced the Generals (1911- 1946), who had replaced Díaz's Cienítficos (1884-1911).

> "No-Nothings" claim to know everything but the opposite is true, and they often turn to thuggery to "enforce" their "wisdom," as did these three "Dirty Presidents" who are infamous in Mexican history.

Claiming to be "Revolutionary" each of these Presidents tried to distribute more land than Lázaro Cárdenas, but most of it was poor land and the use of it contributed to further erosion of the Mexican countryside. By 1982, 'the Official Party cumulatively distributed 42% of Mexico's land surface (compared to Díaz's 32%) to more than 70% of the agriculturally employed population. Many of those Ejidatarios, however, had abandoned their Ejidos to work as day laborers (jornaleros) for a regular pay check with large commercial agricultural enterprises and/or left for the USA to work as braceros. Many moved back and forth between the two countries, depending on seasons. (The number of Braceros working in the USA reached over 5 million between 1942 and 1970.), according to the Booklet of Charts, "History of Mexican Immigration to USA, Chart 39-C.

---

[59] "No-Nothings" claim to know everything but the opposite is true, and they often turn to thuggery to "enforce" their "wisdom," as the three "Dirty Presidents" did in Mexico.

The three Presidents refused to realize that most Ejidos would fail if they were not provided with sufficient agricultural credit (needed to prepare and plant crops) and real agricultural extension (to demonstrate new methods and make available quality seeds as well as fertilizers and insecticides). The three Presidents did, however, plan to provide thousands of tractors for the Mexican countryside in order to increase productivity, but the Ejidatarios and day laborers (many of whom did not have Ejidal rights) blocked the move to tractors on the grounds that machines would put them out of work.

The real problem that GDO, LEA, and JOLOPO faced was that Official Party policy damaged agriculture than through State subsidies for food producers, distributors, and consumers, wasting billions of dollars a year and undermine farm productivity by rewarding inefficiency. For example, The state-run Fertilizantes Mexicanos (FERTIMEx, created by JOLOPO in 1978 by nationalizing all private fertilizer companies), became a government decentralized agency (also called a parastate agency) with a monopoly on production and importation of chemical fertilizers and pesticides, which it operated with such low quality that its products deteriorated in the manufacturing and/or distribution processes.

PRONASE (the National Seed Producing Company) greatly harmed seed quality, forcing many farmers to smuggle seeds into Mexico. PRO- NASE did have quality at the outset under López Mateos, but its rapid expansion under a lazy, inflexible bureaucracy let seeds rot in badly built silos which created conditions of high humidity and inability to prevent attacks on the seeds by rodents (who left their "droppings" to contaminate the stored seeds).

CONASUPO's legendary ability beginning with Lázaro Cárdenas to buy quality agricultural goods from Ejidatarios would be converted by 1970s to paying by the pound, hence in the 1970s farmers added ever more nails and small rocks to their grains as well as "nuts and bolts from discarded machines) to increase weight—only the manufacturers of tortillas and other processed products seemed to care that their food processing equipment would be damaged and food quality would be degraded.

For years official data showed that the Ejidos out produced private agriculture, but only in the 1980s did it begin to become clear that the obverse was true—private producers could only sell to CONASUPO for guaranteed high prices if they sold through Ejidos, which took a percentage to pretend that they were selling to the government. Production statistics, then, confused policy makers who believed that the Ejido was a success. Thus, they had to find out for themselves what Lázaro Cárdenas had known and hidden from the Official Party in 1940—the Ejido had failed to produce for the market. Indeed even as the truth began to be known, it had to be quashed to avoid dispiriting the Party "True Believers" and the Rural Voters needed to keep the Official Party in power.

The Official Party, then, was trapped in its own statistics, which suggested that from 1940 to 1965, Mexico's Ejidal agriculture was at the forefront of the Third World, increasing crop output increasing each year by an average of 6.3%.

But after 1965 agricultural production in Mexico had dropped steadily, primarily because of the inefficiencies caused by increased state intervention in the agrarian economy, according to Thomas E. Cox and Christopher Whalen.[60]

To offset these declines, the State transfers ever more funds to government-operated farm-support agencies, "which reached more than an $2 billion in 1989. Whereas Mexico's agricultural

---

[60] For background, see http://www.heritage.org/Research/LatinAmerica/bg753.cfm

trade surplus before 1970 earned foreign exchange to finance State programs, after 1970 Mexico used foreign loans to pay for money-losing government-owned enterprises and state subsidy programs, including agriculture," as Cox and Whalen tell us.

Mexico's foreign debt in U.S. dollars began to rise under GDO, as we see in Figure 5:

FIGURE 5

Mexico's Real Foreign Debt, 1964-2008

Statism had begun to expand when President Cárdenas used foreign borrowing to expand state power, but this method did not "take-off" until the three Thug Presidents increased borrowing to nationalize ever more private companies as well as to

- subsidize the failing Ejidal sector,
- buy the "support" of Sindicatos in order to prevent popular rebellions,
- feed the cost of corruption as greedy PRI officials demanded to profit from the flow of cash into Mexico.

In December 1964, the foreign debt (the total after adjusting for inflation) stood at US$ 9 billion, and by 1970 it grew to more than $16 billion.

LEA increased this real debt to over $44 billion; and the "honor" for excess goes to JOLOPO, who takes that amount to $144 billion by the time he leaves office in 1982.

To hide the reality of the contradictions and public protest created after 1964, GDO, LEA and JOLOPO secretly launched Mexico's "dirty war" (1964-1978).[61] Although confidential sources

---

61 See the secret files LITEMPO: The CIA's *Eyes on Tlatelolco CIA Spy Operations in Mexico* [1956 1969]: *National Security Archive Electronic Briefing Book No. 204, National Security,* http://www.gwu.edu/~nsarchiv/NSAEBB/NSAEBB204/index.htm

report that Mexico's police, military, and local caciques secretly kidnapped and murdered more than 19,000 persons (labeled as "guerillas)," [62] many of those killed were disgruntled peasants and/or urban intellectuals and workers merely attempting to develop political alternatives to the Official Party. [63]

[FLASH FORWARD: After the PAN captured the presidency via the ballot box in 2000, President Vicente Fox appointed in 2002 a Commission to Investigate the number killed in the Dirty War. This Commission issued a draft report in December 2005, which President Fox feared would prevent the PRI from cooperating with the PAN to form the legislative alliance necessary to achieve legislation being fought by opposition parties, and Fox refused to publish the draft because the Special Prosecutor had suggested it is biased against the government and incomplete because it does not detail the abuses committed by rebel groups. The draft is available with analysis and supporting documents by Kate Doyle: "Draft Report Documents 18 Years of 'Dirty War' in Mexico...State Responsible for [Killings and Disappearances, 1964-1982]."[64] The Commission set out to investigate the deaths 532 persons known to have disappeared out of a total of over 700 persons believed to be missing.[65] Clearly these numbers are too low because entire villages were wiped out and the "War" was fought

---

62 My dates and my estimate based upon interviews with sources who must remain confidential

63 Ibid.

64 http://www.gwu.edu/~nsarchiv/NSAEBB/NSAEBB180/index.htm

65 Cf. "Report on Mexican 'Dirty War' Details Abuse by Military," by Ginger Thompson, Feb. 26, 2006, www.genocidewatch.org/MEXICOReportonMexicanDirty WarDetailsAbusebyMilitaryFeb06.htm

in different parts of Mexico. Just before leaving office, however, Fox approved of a revised version which was put on the internet without public announcement.[66]]

GDO, LEA, and JOLOPO lived by "code" words that had emerged since 1929. Thus, in quoting the code words below, Lorenzo Meyer has stated that "Mexico's contribution to political theory ... is but a footnote" and nothing for which to be proud."

Lorenzo Meyer defines Mexico's reality that applies to actual power in Mexico as involving the following terms: [67]

>'caudillo': powerful national or regional leader;
>'cacique': powerful mid-level or local leader;
>'tapado', the as yet unrevealed Official Party candidate,
>'dedazo', hand picking of political candidates at all levels,
>'mordida': bribe, including authoritarian patronage based on the carrot or the stick;

To this list Lorenzo Meyer might have included (adds PBS):

>'palanca', influence;
>'pezgordo', influential, who is often
>'intocable': untouchable;
>'madrinos', godmothers' (Federal and State Judicial Police, 'commissioned agent-informers,' and fake police), all of whom work for and against the police.

---

[66] See http://www.gwu.edu/~nsarchiv/NSAEBB/NSAEBB209/index.htm and "Mexican Report Cites Leaders for 'Dirty War,' by James C. McKinley, Jr., *New York Times*, Nov. 23, 2006, http://www.nytimes.com/2006/11/23/world/americas/23mexico.html

[67] According to Lorenzo Meyer, the noted historian who teaches at the Colegio de Mexico in Mexico City, quoted in www.pbs.org/wgbh/pages/frontline/shows/mexico/ readings/lupsha.html

12a. President Diaz Ordaz (1964-1970) Initiates Authoritarian Statism

GDO's period marked the shift to the Statist Revolution as the population of Mexico grew from 41 million persons in 1964 to 51 million in 1970.[68]

In the lore propagated by the Official Party, GDO seemed to merit many credits, [69] especially undertaking the construction of Mexico's Metro Rail System, a project vilified by protesters who demanded that funds for such urban development be transferred to the rural sector. [FLASH FORWARD: by the 1990s, GDO's construction of the Metro will be seen as a "stroke of genius," without which by the 2000s Mexico City auto transportation would have smothered with air pollution the entire population of the D.F.]

GDO gained credit from many urban intellectuals for seeking to industrialize rural Mexico and from industrialists and the rural sector for having build 107 dams.

The anti-nuclear weapon activities of GDO led to most nations of the Americas (notably excluding Cuba) signing in 1967 the Treaty of Tlate- lolco, in which they pledge not to acquire such weapons. (A year later, the Plaza would serve as the place of GDO's bloodbath for opposition to PRI that also opposed the holding of the Olympics in Mexico, siphoning resources from the poor in rural Mexico.)

---

[68] Census data reported 48.2 million in 1970.

[69] See Pekka Valtonen, who favorably sums up GDO's contributions, including the promulgation a new Labor Law with the aim of "reforming" work-place problems . Según: www.helsinki.fi/hum/ibero/xaman/articulos/2000_05/valtonen.html

Further, GDO set in motion the development of the la Siderúrgica Lázaro Cárdenas en Las Truchas, Michoacán, planned as a modern steel plant ahead of its times, where he also undertook to build the modern Port of Lázaro Cárdenas.

Behind the scenes, however, Díaz Ordaz and his chief security minister Echeverría initiated their "Dirty War" by having peasant leaders assassinated or kidnapped and killed for protesting the fact that mere land without modern credit and agricultural extension was too often useless. But the protests received little news (usually no news) in the Mexico City media, which was strictly controlled by the PRI. (Local media barely existed in the republic, and was harshly censored through murder of journalists who knew too much for caciques to permit.)

> [FLASH BACKWARD: Some guerrilla leaders had always been killed by local police, such as Rubén Jaramillo who had been guaranteed safety by President López Mateos in 1958 when he abandoned his "war against the PRI. But four years after laying down his weapons, in 1962 Jaramillo was seized along with his wife and three children and all were murdered in cold blood by Morelos state police (aided by a Mexican army officer)—this event causing López Materos to feel shame and revealed the President's lack of control in many areas of the country. The ruthless local PRI caciques, who had seen him as challenging their authority since 1945, when he first rose against them, finally took their revenge to end even his peaceful organization of peasants to protest local abuses.[70]

---

[70] See http://redescolar.ilce.edu.mx/redescolar/publicaciones/publi_quepaso/rubenjaramillo. htm and www.h-net.org/reviews/showpD.F..cgi?path=24155855199874

In 1972, the guerrilla leader Genaro Vázquez will be killed in the State of Guerrero, either by his bad driver (known to be inexpert) or when the state police shot out a tire and caused his car to roll over.[71] Vázquez had founded the Asociación Cívica Guerrerense and the Central Campesina Independiente to politically oppose the Official Party. For these reasons he was seen as en Enemy of the State and imprisoned, but was freed in mid-1968 by his team who were successful to break him out of jail. Henceforth, he left the political arena to convert his movement into the clandestine Asociación Cívica Nacional Revolucionaria, with which he waged (in association with Lucio Cabañas) a "low intensity war" against the PRI's government military forces.[72]

At least the history of Vázquez and Cabañas became partially known to the Mexican public in the 1960s and 1970s because hundreds and hundreds (if not thousands) of such histories did not. Most such cases remained unknown and uncounted, the police and military simply killing or murdering protesters and guerillas, news of such matters being suppressed, which was easy in Mexico's era of rural life without telephone communication and with very poor roads.

Given GDO's penchant for acting with violence and allowing official impunity of action, it was easy for him to make a transition to use mindless brute force against the opposition to the PRI; he

---

[71] Both versions are given in Orlando Ortiz, Genaro Vázquez (México, D.F.: Editorial Diogenes, 1972. Ortiz opens with the last version (which credits police) and closes with the first version (which takes credit from the police).

[72] The history of Genaro Vázquez is not available in the English edition of Wikepedia, but is available in Spanish (and oddly enough in Dutch) editions, http://es.wikipedia. org/wiki/Genaro_Vázquez

was infamous for his mishandling of a number of protests during his term—he fired rail- road workers as well as attacking and firing teachers and IMSS physicians for striking against government corruption and mismanagement of their sectors.

In 1968 GDO ordered the massacre of "student protesters" at the Plaza of Three Cultures (Tlatelolco), [73] his idea being to "assure that Mexico successfully host the Summer Olympic Games" (the first ever held in the Third World). Debate has ensued as to how many students were killed at the Plaza—most estimates varying from 200 to 1,500 student protesters killed—with 300 being the consensus number.[74]

GDO and LEA claimed that students opened fire from building rooftops at the army below at the Plaza of Three Cultures, and we would not know until the Government of Vicente Fox (2000-2006), when government's secret files were opened, that the opening shots were fired by government secret agents firing from the apartment of Lea's sister–in-law.[75]

The 1968 Massacre of "Students" is seen by many as marking yet another the "End of the Mexican Revolution," and "certainly

---

[73] The Three Cultures celebrated in Mexico are Indian-Spanish-Mestizo or Mixed blood.

[74] In realty not all were students. The calculus of those killed has oscillated between 200 y 1,500 (according to reporter Félix Fernández). but the concensus total is 300. Yet Kate Doyle writing in Proceso in 2006 could identify only 44 victims could be found (10 without names) in Mexican government archives opened by President Fox's investigation. www.gwu.edu/~nsarchiv/NSAEBB/NSAEBB201/index.htm

[75] See Reed Johnson and Marla Dickerson, "New Low for Hated Former Leader [Echeverría], *Los Angeles Times,* July 25, 2004.

the end of the Official Party." Actually, as we know, the Official Party did not come to an end until 2000—some 32 years later.

Because the press, television, and radio were so well controlled, the rural and urban murders were swept out of sight and out of mind. Hence, as late as 1967 Mexico was seen as a "development model for the Third World." Brazil's Francisco Julião (the political leader exiled by Brazil's military dictatorship) declared, in my Oral History Interviews with him in Mexico City, that the PRI is an ideal political system because it can maintain order with economic growth but allow criticism by citizens— this only one year before officially-sanctioned murders could no longer be hidden after the above attack on protesters (including many students) at the Plaza of Three Cultures.

The massacre of 1968 (and the later massacre on Corpus Christi Day in 1971) forced protesters to a difficult choice: either join the government or the emerging guerrilla movement. Many opponents of the Official Party went to Cuba to train as guerrillas and re-infiltrate Mexico.

To facilitate the transfer of power from GDO to LEA, the latter insisted in 1970 that as the anointed one to be elected in July to become President of Mexico on December 1 that the students he had arrested (hundreds, if not thousands) be pardoned and that the Law of Social Dissolution be abolished—finally. Too, he gave the vote to eighteen-year olds—a student demand that was a useless one. [76](Ironically GDO got the credit, but the traditional idea of the Official Party required that the outgoing president would make the embarrassing decisions in order so that the new President (in this case LEA) would have an easy a transition as possible. These

---

[76] Ironically, the rights of all citizens to vote were useless until 1997 when the votes of citizens actually were counted in the Mexico City election for Mayor.

transitions were becoming harder to do as the Official Party had become more ruthless in its use of the police powers of the State.)

[FLASH FORWARD: After 1968 the choice of protesters was clear: "Join the government and worked for change from within the Official Party System or join the guerrilla movements.

In 1972, the guerrilla leader Lucio Cabañas was killed in Guerrero state by federal troops. According to Wikipedia:

"Cabañas ... was a Mexican schoolteacher who became a revolutionary, albeit not a Marxist one. Cabañas regarded Emiliano Zapata as his role model and he never abandoned his Christian faith.... He became politically active when he studied at the Guerrero Normal [School to prepare Teachers] and was a leader of the local student union. In 1962 he was elected to the post of General Secretary of the Federation of Socialistic Peasant Students of Mexico.... When [the principal of a] school in Atoyac demanded that all pupils wear school uniforms, Cabañas argued that some families were so poor they could hardly feed their children, not to mention buy school uniforms. [The problem resulted in a strike led by Cabañas against, and ended in shooting and deaths, forcing him to flee to the mountains and join the group of Genaro Vázquez until Vázquez' death in 1972.

"Cabañas established the 'Army of the Poor and Peasant's Brigade Against Injustice.'] They numbered perhaps 300 members and lived in the Guerrero Mountains. He financed his group through kidnappings and bank robberies....

"The Mexican government sent 16,000 soldiers to ... to hunt him. Fifty of them died during the chase.

"In December 1974 Cabañas kidnapped Rubén Figueroa, governor of Guerrero. When the 16,000 government troops sent to track him down tried to rescue the governor, Cabañas committed suicide before being captured.

"Some say Cabañas did not die but ended up in jail. If that was the case he probably would have been executed so that sympathizers would believe the rebellion ended with his death, [thus ending Acapulco's crisis in tourism caused by fear of the Cabañas movement]. There are also numbers of legends about him, including that he had five women bodyguards and carried a bag full of money that he distributed to the poor. Those are most likely 'Tall Tales'; similar legends have been built around Pancho Villa and Emiliano Zapata....

FIGURE 6

Luis Echeverría has just been inaugurated as President by Gustavo Díaz Ordaz(Dec.1, 1970)

SOURCE:http://www.gwu.edu/~nsarchiv/NSAEBB/ NSAEBB204/index.htm (Picture courtesy of Archivo Proceso)

"In recent, years, Cabañas has become a left-wing icon in Mexico, much like Che Guevara and Subcomandante Marcos. During recent social movements, including the 2006 clashes between teachers and the state government of Oaxaca. The face of Cabañas appeared on banners alongside those of Guevara and Vladimir Lenin." [77]

In the meantime, the guerrilla leader Rafael Guillén, the future "Subco- mandante Marcos", trained in Cuba and became a professor in Mexico City to plot rebellion before he went into the jungles of Chiapas from 1984 to 1994. There, he sought to create a Maoist-type movement, according to the masterful history of the Mexico's guerilla movements written by Bernard de la Grange (Le Monde, Paris) and Maite Rico (El País, Madrid).[78] Marcos will emerge only on January 1, 1994, as we will see later.

12b. Luis Echeverria-Alvarez (1970-1976) initiates Economic Statism During LEA's Presidency, the population increased from 51 million in 1970 to 62 million in 1976.

LEA asked himself at the outset why the Government should share profits with private companies. (He failed to realize that the Private Sector generates profits and the Government generates losses.)

> [FLASH FORWARD: LEA's chosen successor, President López -Porti- llo (JOLOPO), at first sought to protect the Private Sector, but after three years will shift to PETRO STATE CAPITALISM, and by 1982 the Central Government will come to own nearly 2,000

---

[77] Quoted from http://en.wikipedia.org/wiki/Lucio_Cabañas

[78] Bernard de la Grange and Maite Rico Marcos, La *Genial Impostura* (México, D.F.: Aguilar, 1997)

Decentralized Agencies (including 1,155 nationally-owed companies), almost all of which operated with deficits and great inefficiency.]

The implicit motto of LEA and JOLOPO was, "The State must take over the major Private Sector, which uses profits for private purposes rather than public good". The seized companies gave two presidents capital that they tended to use not as Public Sector funds but cash for their own private needs and implicit glorious monuments of infrastructure to themselves many of which will crumble in Mexico City's earthquake of 1985 owing to shoddy construction.

Echeverría sought to distance himself from his close relationship with GDO and disavow rumors that both were on the payroll of the CIA. To emphasize this point, he turned away from supporting U.S. policy in the U.N. and on most of its world policy initiatives.

LEA especially moved to expand Mexico's internal State power over an ever-expanding agenda, which always worried the U.S. government and U.S. private investors doing business in Mexico.

To expand the role of the State in Mexico, LEA attempted to set in motion a "legal revolution" with so many new and unworkable laws that few could understand them—see

To carry out the Legal Revolution (as well as to quiet opposition to the Official Party), LEA was determined to place as many academics and intellectuals on the government payroll as possible, this requiring that evermore enterprises be nationalized in order to make places to put his new hires. Professors were given generous grants and higher pay to consult about the new laws and the bureaucracy to make them work as well to keep them busy writing their own studies and books—rather than political tracts.

LEA contributed to the development of Mexico's tourist industry by constructing the world-famous resort city of Cancún based on its pristine beaches. Although he profited by being the God Father for development of tourist industry at Cancún (where only a small village had existed), fortunately he assured protection o the clear water and incredible color of the sea which "changes subtly throughout the day from pale aqua at dawn to deep turquoise at noon to cerulean blue under the blazing afternoon sun to pink-splashed purple during the elegant sunset."[79]

To LEA's discredit, he did not end smoking in Mexico but ended foreign dominance of the tobacco industry by creating the State Tobacco Company (TABAMEx) company 52% owned by the Government, the remaining 48% to be held equally by tobacco companies and farmers.[80] He expanded smoking under government sponsorship.

Unfortunately for Mexico, LEA's "nationalization" of TELMEx in 1972 was supposed to extend service where the private sector had not, but such benefit never came. Perhaps because (a) necessary implementing legislation was delayed until 1974; or (b) new government investment largely went into tapping the telephone of anyone suspected of varying from the Official Party discipline. Indeed LEA justified the nationalization of TELMEx to his security cabinet as giving the PRI greater control to prevent dissent. From 1972 to until its privatization in 1990, government-owned TELMEx continued to make it all but impossible to procure a phone line to one's home or even office without paying huge bribes directly to the telephone installers, who worked on their own rather

---

[79] See www.explorecancun.com/info/beach.shtml

[80] See http://select.nytimes.com/gst/abstract.html?res=F70 914FF3F59107A93C6AB1 78AD95F468785F9

than for the state-telephone monopoly where they were employed. Some joked that "primitive capitalism" was thriving in Mexico.

In reality TELMEx was only partly nationalized and was operated from 1972 to 1990 as a mixed public-private company, with 51% of the shares owned by the government. Although the system nearly completely phased out operators, a customer that requested a telephone line from TELMEx had to wait, "on average, about three years for a hookup. That compared to eight years in Venezuela, but just a few days in the United States, Japan, and most of Europe. In addition, the hookup fee for a single business line could cost $500 or more. Furthermore, at any one time about 10% of all the phone lines in Mexico were out of service. To make matters worse, the government had been increasing long-distance prices (through the tax) at a rapid pace, to the point where the cost of a call had become prohibitive for many customers."[81]

In foreign policy,[82] Echeverría traveled overseas more extensively than any of his predecessors, visiting 35 countries and the Vatican and meeting with 64 heads of government. He established diplomatic relations with 62 nations.

LEA embraced the development concept known as "dependency theory" which argued that Third World countries could achieve economic growth and development only by cutting off their economic and political dependence on the industrialized world, especially the USA. To this end, he established in Mexico City is Center for Third World Studies.

---

[81] See www.funduniverse.com/company-histories/Telefonos-de-Mexico-SA-de-CV- Company-History.html

[82] This discussion draws upon: www.heritage.org/Research/LatinAmerica/bg638.cfm

In 1973, after the overthrow of Allende, Echeverría refused to recognize the new Chilean government, broke diplomatic relations with Chile and welcomed great numbers of leftist refugees from that country. Many Chilean professors who joined the faculty at the National University of Mexico (UNAM) caused havoc by advocating promotions within the University based upon ideology rather than academic research and publication. (Most of the Chilean professors returned home, especially after the dictator Pinochet's lost his 1990 plebe cite to remain in power.)

One of Echeverría's initiatives was the so-called Charter of Economic Rights and Duties approved by the United Nations in 1974 by a vote of 120 to 6, with 10 abstentions. The charter was a collection of Third World complaints and positions blaming industrialized countries as the main cause of economic backwardness. Although it added no new positions, the adoption of the charter by the United Nations gave Echeverría a cause to promote on his trips around the world

In 1975 LEA blundered in his attempt to mediate between Israel and Palestine by stating that he agreed with a proposed U.N. resolution that "zionism is racism." The U.S. Jewish community immediately clamped an embargo on Jewish investment in and tourism to Mexico, which wounded Mexico's economy.

Discovery of giant oil reserves in the Gulf of Mexico was mismanaged by LEA, who sought to keep the find a secret from the USA so that he could use oil as a bargaining chip in his arguments to expand the right for Mexican braceros to gain work permits from the U.S. government and also to gain better treatment of Mexicans living without legal permission in the USA. He feared that the USA would not respond to his demands on immigration matters if it knew about the oil find. In his mind, LEA believed that the U.S. government would demand access to cheap oil as its bargaining chip.

But keeping the oil find a secret was also undermining faith in foreign investors, who were concerned that LEA's spending spree to support his Legal Revolution and State empowerment meant that Mexico had gone from the Era of Development with Stability to an Era of Instability that would eventually bankrupt the country.

The world watched with shock as LEA increased Mexico's total foreign debt in real terms from US$16 billion in 1970 (the year he took office) to $44 billion (the year he left)—see Figure 5, above.

Indeed in late 1976, LEA's expansion of federal expenditure without concern for inflation, meant that he would have to devalued the peso to 20 per dollar, from 12.50 per dollar that had held since 1954—22-yearsof peso stability came to an end. Thus the Official Party lost prestige at home and abroad.

Until his imaginary world of power collapsed in the peso crisis of 1976, LEA had believed that the peso could become the reserve currency to replace the dollar in world economic affairs and that he could become Secretary General of the United Nations. LEA's printing of pesos to raise worker wages backfired, destroying the small gains workers had received, and LEA himself left office in discredit.

12c. José López Portillo (1976-1982), Petro-Statism Under "God JOLOPO"

Under JOLOPO, the population of Mexico grew from 62 million in 1976 to 73 million in 1982.

Taking power in December 1976, JOLOPO had to major goals:
    a. establish the National Family Planning Program to aggressively reduce Mexico's high total fertility rate, which stood at 7.0 (from 1950 to 1970). This

Program was one of JOLOPO's few real successes.[83] The change in attitude to help Mexicans understand the country was no longer "under populated", the issue that Lázaro Cardenas had seen as a major problem during his presidency. JOLOPO's efforts paid dividends as the fertility rate decreased to 4.2 (for the five-year average from 1980 to 1985), and 2.5 (2000-2005).

b. restore the confidence of the Private Sector, which had feared investing in LEA's bubble economy.

Thus, during his first 3 years in office, JOLOPO set out to develop an Alliance with the Private Sector and to create growth poles in all corners of the country by using tax incentives.

But with Arab oil money flowing into Mexico to develop PEMEx via New York banks (who were paid outrageous commissions and who received enormous "kickbacks") especially during the last 3 years in office, JOLOPO decided that he was himself God. He saw himself as Quetzalcóatl, the Aztec's most "beneficent" God who had left across the sea to the East, [84] but who "promised to return" when needed; and in his madness of wild expenditure (e.g. on pipelines for oil and gas leading nowhere), "God JOLOPO", now arrogant and pompous, put Mexico on the road to bankruptcy/

---

[83] **The rate had stood at 6.9 in 1955**. See U.N. chart in first source, below: http:// globalis.gvu.unu.edu/indicator_detail.cfm?IndicatorID=138&Country=MX www. country-data.com/cgi-bin/query/r-8721. html www.airninja.com/worlD.F.acts/ countries/Mexico/fertilityrate.htm

[84] Cortés victory over the Aztecs was was facilitated by the fact that Moctezuma originally thought in 1519 that Cortés was Quetzalcóatl, in Aztec mythology the first chief of the dynasty, who would return from the Orient and retake power. Moctezuma had ordered the coast at Veracruz to be watched. See http://virtualology.com/apmontezuma/

JOLOPO's Petro-Statism used the income from the quintupling of oil prices (caused by two OPEC oil embargos against the USA) to curtail further the partnership of private companies owned jointly since the 1940s by U.S. and Mexican investors as well as to end many partner- ships that had emerged since the 1960s between the Government and the Private Sector.

NAFINSA (the National Development Bank) had gradually taken over parts of the Mexican steel industry.[85] Altos Hornos (AHMSA, Mexico's first plant dating from 1900) was absorbed after World War II; the Fundidora Monterrey was taken over by NAFINSA in the crisis caused by LEA's devaluation of the peso in 1976: and in 1978 JOLOPO decided to nationalize the steel mill at Port Lázaro Cárdenas in the state of Michoacán (Siderúrgica Lázaro Cárdenas Las Truchas). To do the latter, he cre- 84 Cortés victory over the Aztecs was was facilitated by the fact that Moctezuma originally thought in 1519 that Cortés was Quetzalcóatl, in Aztec mythology the first chief of the dynasty, who would return from the Orient and retake power. Moctezuma had ordered the coast at Veracruz to be watched. See http://virtualology.com/ apmontezuma/85 See www.ipab.org.mx/01_acerca_ipab/origen. html and www.economia.unam.mx/ publicaciones/econunam/ pD.F.s/09/04EmilioSacristan.pD.F. ated SIDERMEx as a holding company to administer it along with the plants "owned" by NAFINSA. The whole scheme collapsed in JOLOPO's devaluation of the peso in 1982, but privatization would not come until 1991.

By the death of JOLOPO's crazy-style Statism, the government of Mexico owned 1,155 enterprises—the great majority operated as inefficient, over-staffed state monopolies. When JOLOPO left office, no one knew how many of these enterprises even existed.

---

[85] See www.ipab.org.mx/01_acerca_ipab/origen.html and www.economia. unam.mx/ publicaciones/econunam/pD.F.s/09/04EmilioSacristan.pD.F.

That would come out in the international audit of Mexico's assets by creditors from around the world.

JALOPO astounded Mexico the world by taking Mexico's foreign debt from a relatively small US$44 billion (when he took office in 1976) to a huge $144 billion in 1982. When the world oil price collapsed in 1982, JOLOPO could not make payments on the debt, Mexico found itself bankruptcy, where upon he nationalized the private banks, trying to blame them for his mess. True, customers of the banks (including himself) had shifted money out of the country to avoid the inflation that he had caused, but self-preservation was not illegal until he made it so—but only after he had put his money into property and banks in Coronado Beach, California.

The devaluation of the peso in 1982 made it costly to buy one U.S. dollar: 96.5 pesos.

Needless to say, JOLOPO's reputation was ruined in 1982, long before revelations that he had as President ordered genocide in the "Dirty War." Thus, he would go down in history (along with LEA) as having been a "monstrous leader" of Mexico.

13. RISE OF ACTIVE-STATISM, 1983—

13a. Carlos Salinas (implicitly 1983-1988; and explicitly 1988-1994) lay basis for the 3 presidents who have followed him when the Active-State wing of the Official Partly wins control of the PRI-Gobierno:

The population of Mexico rose from 75 million in 1983 to 90 million in 1994, during which time Dr. Carlos Salinas de Gortari (PHD, Harvard University), effectively becomes President of Mexico for two terms (1982-1994), and bringing into position the generation of the "techno- crats". This word has a negative connotation in English, but in Spanish "técnicos" has a positive one, if laced with irony as time has gone on under those with higher studies in the USA.

Ironically, as Secretary of Programming and Budget (1982-1987), Salinas built into that ministry coordinated control reaching into every aspect of government that gave him more control over the economy and society control than the "nominal" President Miguel de la Madrid, under whom GSG served and the virtual President.

Nominal President Lic. de la Madrid (Dec. 1982-Dec. 1988), who had received his M.A. from Harvard University, now, as President, mainly concerned himself with political and ceremonial matters. In Salinas second term, he was President in his own right (De. 1988-Dec. 1994), and take full control of politics as well.

In 1983 Salinas had to immediately face the problem of the foreign debt. He "solved" it when he appointed Dr. Ernesto Zedillo, a young professor of economics at El Colegio de México, to drew upon his expertise gained at Yale University. Having written his PHD dissertation on Mexico's foreign debt, Zedillo came up the plan for stretching out the debt problem in order save the Private Sector, which owned millions that it could not pay to foreign banks and lenders, as did the autonomous agencies, which had quietly each borrowed abroad on the basis that their loans would be backed by the federal government of Mexico. Unfortunately, the extent of the decentralized debt was unknown to Mexico's Minister of Treasury, and nobody knew the extent of the problem, let alone how many auton- omous agencies even existed. The IMF, foreign governments, and foreign lenders demanded an audit to determine the debts and assets of the Central and Decentralized Governments. No one wanted this information more than Salinas, who needed to know the extent of the economic mess left by JOLOPO.

Thus, the government took over all "valid" private-sector foreign debts and some domestic debt to negotiate a settlement that creditors only be repaid over time through a government "debt-holding fund", in 1984 officially named FONAPRE , and eventually called FOBAPROA (1990) and then IPAB (1999).

> [FLASH FORWARD: IPAB will be set up to manage the fall- out from the Peso Crisis of 1994-1995.86
> And, unfortunately for Salinas, Zedillo could not abolish the accumulated real foreign debt of US$ 144 billion in 1982, which drained the ability of Mexico to invest in the country's development. In 1988 the real foreign debt had declined to
> $129 billion, and in 1994 rise to US$ 155 billion. During 1995, Zedillo's first full year in office as President, the real foreign debt would balloon to US$ 177 billion. For the long- term series on nominal and real data for Mexico's foreign debt, see Figure 5.]

Yet Salinas and his financial advisor Zedillo (working at the Bank of Mexico, 1983-1987; and Treasury Ministry, 1987-1992) had saved private capitalism in Mexico from going bankrupt, and the joke was on JOLOPO, who thought that he had once-and-for-all wiped out the Private Sector.

But JOLOPO did cause havoc and a ten-year battle for Salinas to right the country after he wrecked its policymaking machine when he nationalized the private banks in 1982 to attack his "enemies" who were "guilty" of having destroyed the Mexican economy to spite his role as "God." JOLOPO's infantile attack on the Private Sector is akin to Hitler's plan to flood the subways to kill innocent women, children, and the aged for not having taken up arms to

---

[86] Some observers have suggested, tongue-in-cheek, that Zedillo should now be called from his current post at head of Yale's Globalization Center to apply his Mexican debt solution of the 1980's to the U.S. credit meltdown of 2008-2010.

prevent Russia's capture of Berlin in 1945. At least Hitler failed in that vengeance—JOLOPO did succeed in harming Mexico's development .

> [FLASH FORWARD: In late 1992, US$ 1 was worth 3,175 pesos before Salinas could stabilize inflation and expenditure. At that point and after a ten-year battle he was able to convert the exchange rate to US$ 1 to 3.17 pesos, as of January 1, 1993.[87]]

The need to reign government spending (and thus inflation) was compli- cated by the 1985 earthquake that destroyed much of downtown Mexico City, leading to thousands of deaths. "President" Miguel la Madrid was paralyzed by the death and destruction, and unable to assume any leadership role, which placed more burden on Salinas than he already had assumed to strengthen the national recovery process.

The bright side of the earthquake was that for the first time in Mexican history the population had to assume leadership in its own right without waiting for orders from the government, the military, or the police. Mexico City's population shifted from passive civil society (which mainly votes for others) to active Civic Society. The Civic role here involved joining with others to begin the rescue process, marshal water brigades to put out fires and connect electricity to areas without the ability to survive otherwise. The populace formed itself to "police" the affected areas against looting and served to direct traffic as well as arrange for food supplies to be distributed.

---

[87] See www.nytimes.com/1992/12/20/travel/travel-advisory-new-peso-for-mexico-on- jan-1.html Cf. the IMF peso series, which converts data for its long-term series for Mexico as of 1986.

Inflation and expenditure problems complicated Salinas's need to get Mexico City functioning after that massive 1985 earthquake.

Unfortunately for Mexico and the USA, 1985 was the year in which both countries realized how serious drug violence in Mexico had become. U.S. DEA agent Enrique Camarena was kidnapped in broad daylight in Gua-dalajara, tortured, and then executed by drug dealers.[88] He had infiltrated drug trafficking rings and successfully helped break up many of them. He managed to keep his face out the newspapers even though his name was well known. One of the groups he was following managed to identify and execute him.

The DEA, working with Mexican police, identified two Mexican citizens as suspects the Camarena torture-murder case: i) Humberto Álvarez-Machaín, the physician who allegedly prolonged Camarena's life so the torture could continue, and ii) Javier Vásquez-Velasco. Because of Mexican legal barriers to extradition, U.S. agents kidnapped and took them to the USA. Despite vigorous protests from the Mexican government, Álvarez was tried in United States District Court in Los Angeles. The trial resulted in an acquittal. Vásquez-Velasco was arrested for his alleged involvement in the murder and sentenced to three life sentences.

By tending to ignore the illegal drug trade, elements of the PRI seemingly reached accommodations with many drug lords, and Raúl Salinas de Gortari (brother of Virtual President Carlos Salinas) would eventually be linked to some of them as his "generous friends." PBS gives many sources linking Raúl to Documents from the Office of Mexico's Attorney General and the National

---

[88] The following draws upon http://en.wikipedia.org/wiki/Enrique_Camarena

Anti-Drug Institute revealing that Raul Salinas had ties with drug lords in Mexico as early as 1987.[89]

led by Joaquin "El Chapo" Guzman-Loera,[90] and (ii) the Gulf Cartel's Juan Garcia-Abrego (whose uncle founded this cartel in the 1970 to smuggle whiskey into Mexico before Juan moved into smuggling drugs into USA in the 1980s). According to one of the documents, Raúl Salinas had guaranteed protection to the Juan García-Abrego at the time Carlos Salinas was candidate in 1987 to become president in his own name.[91]

Meanwhile, "President" de la Madrid alienated the PRI's "Democratic Current" led by Cuauhtémoc Cárdenas-Solorzano (CCS, the son of Lázaro) and Porfirio Munõz—Ledo, who were "forced" to leave the PRI in 1987. They founded Mexico's Democratic Front (forerunner of the PRD - see below) in their struggle to defeat at the polls Salinas' PRI, which had turned against their cherished Statism.

Cuauhtémoc Cárdenas actually won the election of 1988, according to the vote-count trend established before the "computers crashed" to reveal that the PRI had lost. Cuauhtémoc apparently

---

[89] See http://www.pbs.org/wgbh/pages/frontline/shows/ico/news/reforma.html

[90] During the 1980s, El Chapo (which means "Shorty", in English) was air traffic coordinator for Miguel Ángel Félix-Gallardo (known as "The Godfather" of al; narcotraficantes and as "Lord of the Skies" ("El Señor de los Cielos") because he was the first to use air transport of drugs in major way), head of the dominant drug trafficking group in Mexico at that time. After Félix Gallardo's capture in 1989 (http://www.encyclopedia.com/doc/1P2-1184588.html), El Chapo Guzmán began taking control of the organization and soon gained notoriety as director of the Sinaloa Cartel. See discussion at 13d.2, below.

[91] Juan was captured in 1996 and is currently serving eleven life terms in a maximum- security federal prison in Colorado.

made a secret with deal Carlos Salinas about which we know little except that it was hidden from Porfirio Munõz-Ledo (President of the nascent the PRD), and the deal allowed Carlos Salinas to take power. Because the central-election-com- puter crash (which we now know was faked) prevented the vote count from being verified in the time limits established by law, Cuauhtémoc either felt that he did not want to create a crisis that could lead to blood- shed

Government and its Sindicatos as well as the role of Sindicatos in many private companies.

Although much has dismantlement has taken place since 1983, in 1994, and still in 2010, the Corporativist system still wields major power in all decisions of State.

Beginning in 1983, Salinas led a Counter-Revolution from within the Official Party of the Revolution. Salinas ended the ever-rising power of the State by ending excessive societal regulation, even as he accumulated centralized political power for himself. After having recognized the failure of Statism, wherein the Central Government and its decentralized agencies had come to control more than half (perhaps 60%) of the GDP of Mexico as well as heavily regulate all private activity, Anti-Statism was Salinas major focus at first but soon shifted to Active Statism—after a wave of selling-off government industries, especially the telephone system that was sold for a pittance to Carlos Slim (who parlayed that company's implicit wealth into his personal fortune to become the richest person in the world).

1989: For his own Presidential campaign, Salinas used his intellectual background, to justify his role which called for liberalizing the economy while protecting people who were not in a position to protect themselves (the unemployable, the disabled, the aged, the children in need, etc.)— he called this approach "Social Liberalism" to distinguish it from U.S. Liberalism and to avoid any debate about the role of the Active State and Anti-State policy. (The idea of "Social Liberalism" was extensively revived in Europe and has since become a basis for the European Union as decentralized Active State.)

To implement his ideology, Salinas established his system of "Solidarity."[92] The National Solidarity Program (PRONASOL) that granted funds to communities for projects that they need (schools, clinics, bridges, irriga-tion systems, etc.), provided that they do the work themselves or volunteer to help outside companies do specialized aspect. Further, community leadership will have to collectively oversee expenditures to expand their civic consciousness and civic demands upon the central government in Mexico City.

This marks Salina's shift from Anti-Statism to reestablishing the "Active State" under a different name.

Immediately after taking office as President in his own right, Salinas recognizes the election in Baja California of Ernesto Ruffo-Appel, the first opposition governor—a member of PAN.

On the crime front, although narcotraficante Miguel Ángel Félix-Gal- lardo, the "God Father" and Capo of the Guadalajara Cartel was arrested and incarcerated in 1989, he remained one of Mexico's major traffickers, maintaining his organization via cell phone from prison until he was transferred to a new maximum security prison in the 1990s. At that point, his Guadalajara Cartel, broke up into two factions: the Tijuana Cartel led by his nephews (the Arellano Félix brothers), and the Sinaloa Cartel (run by former

---

[92] Two views with excellent data are: a generally positive analysis, see www.jstor.org/pss/3185151 and a generally negative one, see www.questia.com/googleScholar.qst?docId=98486401

lieutenants Héctor Luis Palma Salazar, Adrián Gómez González and El Chapa Joaquín Guzmán).[93]

On the economic front, in 1989 Salinas oversaw the sale of Dina to a Guadalajara entrepreneur, who turned it into a money-making operation. In 1994 the private company became the largest bus manufacturer in North America.

In 1990 Salinas reduced the number of "strategic" industries such as coal mining and he permitted up to 100% foreign capital investments, except in the few remaining strategic industries (such as petroleum, electricity, and airlines). For all foreign investment in industry he announced that if his government did not disapprove or approve of its plan within 30 days after receiving it, the plan was approved—automatically.

Salinas re-privatized the banks in 1992, eight years two late to prevent the government-owned banks from having made loans to PRI friends, then forgiving the loans as bad debts. Further, the government banks had failed to invest in modern technology being adopted banks around the world. These problems hampered Salinas massive sale of the PRI- Government's state-owed industries, which not only were inefficient but losing huge amounts of money.

Salinas had already begun massive privatizations, such as the government telephone monopoly in 1990, which went to Carlos Slim, who promised to offer more extensive and better service but forgot to say that he would by charging the world's highest telephone rates.[94](How can small Mexican business complete

---

[93] See http://en.wikipedia.org/wiki/Miguel_Caro_Quintero

[94] CSG enabled Slim to buy TELMEx at an artificially low cost and pay for it over time using money earned by the phone service, enabling Slim to build his fortune and become in the 21st century the world's richest person. "After privatization, TELMEx began

with their counterparts in the USA, who pay half the cost that Slim charges.)

Although Salinas privatized mineral resources in 1993, except for PEMEx, he did not propose to privatize the State electrical agency, which in Statist mythology is almost as important as PEMEx.

In 1992 Salinas "privatized" Ejido lands by enticing Congress and the states legislatures to change the Constitution of 1917 in order to begin granting individual titles so that Ejidatarios could make their own decisions about their land—rent it, sell, put it up for collateral to borrow money, or even hold it to be inherited by their family (all hitherto illegal). Very little Ejido land has been sold because of its poor soil, except in isolated cases.

Further, Salinas made peace with the Church in 1992, obtaining congressional approval for its right recover their Churches and own property that had been nationalized. Further, the new Salinas law granted the Church to right to conduct religious education and legally hold public ceremonies. Henceforth, priests have been considered normal citizens with the right to vote. Last, but not least, Mexico reestablished diplomatic relations with the Vatican after 130 years, [95] relations having been broken in 1862.

CSG had begun privatization of the failed State agricultural enterprises such as PRONASE in 1989 as well as FERTIMEx and

---

investing in new, modern infrastructure, creating a nationwide optic fiber network, and offering service in most of the country," according to http://en.wikipedia. org/wiki/TELMEx

[95] "While some powers were reinstated by the dictator Porfirio Díaz before his overthrow by the revolutionaries, Mexican leaders and the Pope continued to exchange only temporary or ' lower-level envoys," according to Tim Golden, "Mexico and the Catholic ChurchRestore Full Diplomatic Ties," New York Times, September 22, 1992.

ANDSA in 1991—PRONASE being infamous for jeopardizing Mexico's production of seeds (not to mention ending the production of quality seeds), ANDSA bring scandalous for its decrepit silos and filthy, fungus-ridden- crop depositories, and FERTIMEx being criticized for having provided degraded fertilizers and pesticides too often to late to be of use. All of these agencies wasted subsidies on inefficient operations that harmed the nation's food supply and food producing equipment. Bureaucrats and Sindicato workers shrugged their shoulders and said: "Efficiency, quality, and cleanliness are the responsibility of someone else—who knows who."

Salinas privatized TABAMEx in 1990 when the government was trying to stimulate public health. However, the foreign buyers insisted that the government "get rid" of the huge stockpile of foul quality tobacco that had been accumulated over the years by TABAMEx. The stockpile was bad from its start because the government paid growers for quantity not quality, and the producers had taken advantage to "unload" it on the government, apparently convincing themselves if that if their sickening tobacco did get into cigarettes and cigars that would matter—smokers are going die form smoking anyway.

Once having purchasing so much bad tobacco, TABAMEx stored it improperly. Because the mess of rotting tobacco was too heavy to move (and where could it even be moved was a quandary), the government decided to burn the stinking mess, a mistake which contaminated the air of central Mexico for many days. It was a real "smoke-out", joked critics who laughed and coughed at the same time. People who had given up smoking had a last round of unwanted coughs.

In the meantime, CONASUPO's LICONSA (which sells "milk" in ugly tasting grey powder to be reconstituted usually with unsanitary tap water) was recreated as a company with the majority of shares owned by the State. From 1944 to 1994 it had been wholly owned by the government. With the in rise prices received by producer, LICONSA could shift some subsidies to the consumption side and encourage consumers not to waste milk supplies.

In the same manner as LICONSA was reorganized as a mixed State- private company in 1994, DICONSA followed suit. Unfortunately for many small DICONSA trucks would no longer reach isolated communities, the economic cost being considered too high. Not until 2005, however, did DICONSA begin to modernize its warehouses, 300 operating its national network that a technological upgrade to communicate with suppliers, trucks, and DICONSA distribution points to consumers as well to prevent food supplies from expiring.[96]

Salinas' programs ended high tariffs and opened Mexico to Free Trade Agreements (FTAs) with countries around the world. His first and most important FTA was signed in 1993 with the USA and Canada and named

"NAFTA" (North American Free Trade Area), which went into effect January 1, 1994. Treaties with the European Union and Central America followed. (In 2003 Mexico would serve as the Presidency of the nascent 21 Asia-Pacific Economic Countries (APEC), including countries such as Vietnam which are not Pacific Ocean countries.[97]

---

[96] On the situation of DICONSA attempts to modernize in 2005 under President Fox, see www2.gxtechnical.com/portal/hgxpp001.aspx?15,7,3, O,E,0,PAG;CONC;151;4; D;10145;1;PAG;MNU;E;25;3;5;12;MNU

[97] See Olga Magdalena Lazín, *La globalización se descentraliza. Libre mercado, Fundaciones, Sociedad Cívica y Gobierno Civil en las Regiones del Mundo.* (Guadalajara, Los Ángeles, México: Universidad de Guadalajara, UCLAProgram on Mexico, PROFMEX/ WORLD, Casa Juan Pablos Centro Cultural, 2007). Prólogo de James W. Wilkie.

In the meantime, Subcomandante Marcos, hidden in Chiapas with his Maoist-oriented guerrilla force named the Ejército zapatista de Liberación Nacional (EzLN) since 1983, had grown frustrated with Coman- dante Germán, his superior in Mexico City. Germán had held Marcos in check for years by arguing that "the time was not ripe to launch the Revolution against the PRI-Gobierno. But NAFTA gave Marcos the spark he needed to ignore Germán's orders and begin in Chiapas the national uprising of Indigenous "Indigenous and oppressed peoples" to overthrow the PRI-Gobierno.

Subcomandante Marcos used the inauguration of NAFTA on January 1, 1994, as offering the opportunity to finally ignore the orders of Coman- dante Germán. That first day of 1994, then, Marcos unleashed his attack on the PRI-Government by capturing San Cristóbal de las Casas, gaining propaganda points by claiming (falsely, but effectively) that was his main goal was to protest against NAFTA. In reality, he and Comandante saw their main goal as gaining Indigenous autonomy within Mexico by establishing a Revolutionary Government that would spread to all of Mexico.

That the EzLN had remained hidden, as had the Dirty War, escaped the attention of the otherwise very perceptive Mario Vargas-Llosa (the famous Peruvian novelist and one-time presidential candidate). Thus, he was able to proclaim in 1990 the PRI to be "La Dictadura Perfecta," because it allowed dissent while successfully developing the Mexican nation. Like Julião before him, he did not realize that the Dirty War even existed in Mexico whereas Argentines, Brazilians, Chileans, and Uruguayans all knew the open fact of Dirty War being conducted as it took place in their countries.

Subcomandante Marcos proved that his experience as one time professor of communications at the University of Mexico City would save the EzLN. Marcos launched an Internet campaign to inform the world of the EzLN goals and seek protection from civic society around the globe, especially in the USA and Europe. The result of the first Internet campaign by guerrillas anywhere brought so many much bad publicity about the campaign of the Mexican army against the EzLN that Salinas halted attacks and permitted Marcos to organize a major part of the state of Chiapas.

Civic society from around the world wired funds to the EzLN bank accounts in Mexico—another permission granted by Salinas. Marcos was thus free to organize his own view of utopian activity based in communities called "caracoles" (snails), and they proceeded, as Marcos announced, to organize at a snail's pace that would in the end prove that slow, steady activity can outshine fast-paced development without real humanity.

In fact Marcos created is own prison from which he later negotiated with the Fox government to consider changes in Mexico's Constitution of 1917 to let the Indigenous people be a state within the State, a nation within the Nation of Mexico. Marcos ideas appealed to many non-Indians until they realized that the Indigenous law would be based on "usos y costumbres" with its unfortunate suppression of women's' rights and arbitrary justice being imposed differently according to region and without appeal. Hence the idea of a separate Indian nation within Mexico passed (which surfaces from time to time) again faded into the background.

Marcos himself seemed not to have understood the real struggle in Chiapas involved the one between Protestants and the Catholics over who should interpret the true faith to the Indians and the extent to which the Bible could be interpreted by the religious leaders and their followers. Further, the Protestant attempt to end the use of alcohol by caciques to control male workers won over many Indigenous women; hence the Roman Catholic Church realized that if it did not want to be displaced it would have to join the movement against the use of alcohol as a control mechanism, which in any case was (and is) perverting simple justice from being rendered by and rational argument among inebriated tribal elders.

However, the caciques who prefer to keep Indian males in a drunken stupor, have supported establishment of the Mexican Catholic Church to subvert the Roman Catholic Church. Violence periodically erupts at San Juan Chamula as these three religious groups fight over who should control the church there, and more than 20,000 Indians have had to flee to other areas to avoid being physically beaten in this competition four souls and struggle over the use of alcohol. The Mexican Indian Institute established in 1948 (but abolished by President Fox) in 2003 to establish a Commission for the Development of Indigenous Peoples)98 [98]unwise refused to take a position on alcohol, concerned that it would interfere in Indian rights to make tribal decisions while under the historic use of alcohol.

CSG found that the Marcos uprising on January 1, 1994, was just the beginning of his problems because two mysterious assassinations of PRI- Gobierno leaders added an unheard of dimension in high-level Mexican politics. In March of 1994, CSG's choice of president to succeed him, Luis Donaldo Colosio was assassinated, causing a political crisis.

In September 1994, the PRI Secretary General José Francisco Ruiz Mas- sieu (the brother-in-law of GSG), was assassinated, probably by drug dealers involved with CSG's brother Raúl.

---

[98] See http://www.e-mexico.gob.mx/wb2/eMex/
eMex_Instituto_Nacional_Indigenista_sit

[FLASH FORWARD: Raúl was later sentenced under the Zedillo government to over 27 years in prison for his supposed part in the assassination of Ruiz Massieu.[99] Because Raúl's conviction was driven by a fever of hatred, ignited by President Zedillo against the Salinas clan to shift blame from himself for having "caused" the peso crisis of 1994, Raúl appealed to Mexico's Supreme Court, and under Fox his conviction was reversed. Raúl's ten years in prison seemed as if "poetic justice" had its day in Mexico.][100]

13b. Active-Statist Revolution Under President Ernesto Zedillo (1994- 2000), who agrees to count the votes fairly and when the PRI loses the Presidency in 2000, he turns the government over to PAN's Vicente Fox Under Zedillo the population rose from 90 million in 1995 to 99 million in 2000,[101] depending on the time of year when Mexicans return to work during the U.S. rainy, cold season.

Indeed, Salinas overcame the assassination of the PRI presidential candidate Luis Donaldo Colosio in 1994 by stage-managing the election of Ernesto Zedillo as President of Mexico, 1994-2000.

Salinas himself seemed headed to become President of the new World Trade Organization (1995—), but that route was cut-off when Zedillo named Dr. Jaime Serra Puche (PHD, Yale University) as Minister of the Treasury.

---

[99] See http://en.wikipedia.org/wiki/Jos%C3%A9_Francisco_Ruiz_Massieu

[100] Raúl was arrested Feb. 28, 1995, and released from prison on June 14, 2005.

[101] The census gave 97.5 million. Projections from the 1970s forecast that, given the 7.0 fertility rate, in 2000 Mexico would surpass132 million persons—See Wilkie, ed. SALA, Vol. 19 (1978), Table 622.

Serra's own arrogant incompetence caused an unwarranted peso panic beginning in December 1994. Serra, who thought himself so important as the next President of Mexico (still six years in the future) that he not deign to call New York and London bankers with weekly updates that all was well in Mexican finances—as his predecessor Dr. Pedro Aspe had done. Having fired Aspe's entire staff, Serra did not know which levers actually worked at Treasury, and as foreign banks pulled out capital, the peso collapsed, with the real foreign debt standing at US$ 155 billion (up from real US$ 129 billion when Salinas had taken office.

Mexico was "saved" in 1995 when a) Zedillo replaced the failed Serra with Guillermo Ortiz (today Governor of the Bank of Mexico), and b) President Bill Clinton organized a financial rescue package102[102] of US$ 55 billion in real terms (involving US$ 33 billion in real terms from the USA and the rest from the IMF and Canada—debt which was repaid early.)[103]

In his memoirs, Salinas writes (without naming names) about having been defeated by such Official Party "hacks" (presumably including Serra), who belong to the Mexican nomenklatura— the Russian colloquial term for high professional functionaries of the government, especially the apparatchik types who hold positions of bureaucratic or political responsibility. Members of the "apparat" are frequently transferred between different areas of responsibility, usually with little or no actual training for their

---

[102] The resulting U.S. rescue of Mexico by the Clinton Administration was wrongly criticized by www.heritage.org/Research/LatinAmerica/bg1016.cfm

[103] In nominal terms the rescue package totaled $50 billion (of which $30 billion wasU.S. funding).

new areas of responsibility. Thus, the term apparatchik, or "agent of the apparatus" is usually the best possible description of the person's profession and occupation. Today this term is also used in contexts other than Russia. For example, it is often used to describe people who cause bureaucratic bottlenecks in otherwise efficient organizations, especially at support services groups such as critical information technology (IT) services.[104]

Many observers of Mexico have called the leaders since Salinas' influence beginning in 1983 as the "Generación de los Técnicos", subliminally recalling the "Científicos" who had helped Porfirio Díaz govern Mexico from 1884 to 1911 the second part of his Díaz's 34 years in power. Both terms have been used to derogate their roles, although all agree that they were better than the period of the "No-Nothing Thugs", 1965-1982. The generations of the Generals in power (1911-1946) and the Lawyers (1946-1964) had relied on many técnicos for advice and to staff the government, but since Salinas they came into power.

Although Zedillo made Salinas the scapegoat for Serra's errors, Zedillo continued the Salinas Programs of signing new FTAs around the world as well as well as developing revised FTAs to improve the first round of FTAs that had been signed by President Salinas.

President Zedillo

    a. privatized petrochemical industries;
    b. privatized Mexican social security accounts in 1997;[105]

---

[104] Forfurtherdiscussion,seehttp://en.wikipedia.org/wiki/Nomenklatura#The_New_Class and http://en.wikipedia.org/wiki/Apparatchik

[105] The Wall Street Journal reported in 1999: "Since the implementation of Mexico's private pension system on July 1, 1997, about 14.5 million Mexican workers have opened their own pension savings accounts." See WSJ article reprinted at: http://www. cato.org/pub_display.php?pub_id=5032

c. re-privatized the Mexican National Railway "System" in 1998, reviving an industry that had become moribund and dangerously decrepit under State mismanagement;

d. closed CONASUPO, which had been difficult to close by Salinas because the poor population (both rural and urban) had come to depend on its cheap food, regardless of quality; and farmers were able to sell as guaranteed prices, also regardless of quality. Zedillo could finally close CONASUPO in 1999, the State shifting to focus on quality of food, not quantity. The State had finally lost all patience (as had consumers) with the bureaucratic thicket of mismanaged that CONASUPO had come to represent.[106] In the end, although much food arrived, it did with expired dates—old and stale.

Thus, as CONASUPO was closed by Zedillo (the rotten CONASUPO model could not be sold as no company would buy into its complete failure), Zedillo, using my wording announced in Mexico the success of "Mexico's Second Green Agricultural Revolution for the World."

The Second Green Agricultural Revolution made by Norman Borlaug (who made the First Green Agricultural Revolution—see Part 11b, above), would not be announced in until May 1999, when President Zedillo and I joined Borlaug to announce in Mexico City the development of "double-protein corn" and recognize Mexico's role in the process begun in 1944. Although the improvement of corn had been planned as part of the First Green Agricultural

---

[106] To understand the incredible bureaucracy created by CONASUPO, see Enrique C. Ochoa, *Feeding Mexico: The Political Uses of Food since* 1910 (Wilmington, Deleware: Scholarly Resources, 2000).

Revolution (which did include successfully the improvement of rice in the Philippines as an off-shoot of Borlaug's work in Mexico), research with corn took decades because of the complexity of the problem. Indeed, the International Advisory Board that had taken over CIMMyT from the Mexican Government decided in 1988 that the goal of creating Quality Protein Maize would never be reached, cut off his funding, and closed CIMMyT, except to maintain its World Seed Bank.

With new funding, from Japan's Sasakawa Foundation, [107]Borlaug moved his Mexican Corn Research Team to Ghana, their long-research finally coming to fruition by the late 1990s. Ironically, Mexico's Ejidatarios have been glacially slow to adopt the new corn seeds whereas Brazilian and Chinese farmer have rapidly adopted it. (Hogs fed double-protein corn, for example, then to be up to twice as big compared to those fed with normal corn.)

In 1999 Zedillo invited Norman E. Borlaug and his Mexican Research Team to return to Mexico, where the Mexican Government reopened CIMMyT for their continued research to expand the Second Green Agricultural Revolution (AgGreen), which originated in Mexico. At the event with Zedillo, hosted by Roberto González-Barrera (RGB) and his GRUMA corporation , I was invited to present my view ("The Wilkie View") in which there are two parallel strands: a) Borlaug has developed seeds from his original base in Mexico; and b) RGB has developed super corn tortillas with vitamins and minerals for the masses from his original base in Mexico.

Borlaug and RGB both recognize the importance of high-protein, low- carb diets that can prevent weight gain that leads to diabetes. Borlaug now seeks to implant in Mexico the high-protein

---

[107] See http://www.worlD.F.oodprize.org/borlaug/borlaug-history.htm

corn seeds (which are already planted in Brazil and China but not in Mexico) that RGB needs to make the tortilla ever more healthy.

For the Second AgGreen Revolution, Borlaug's long search for renewable seeds came to fruition in the lab (then the fields) when he created seeds that are resistant to drought and disease but use less chemical fertilizers, herbicides, fungicides, and pesticides. This was possible through targeted genetic transformation of corn seeds in the lab (which takes weeks, not the decades of his work on wheat).

Whereas the First AgGreen Revolution had to use untargeted and waste- ful transformation of whole gene pools through time consuming hybrid plant development by trial and error, the Second has been able to take advantage of targeted research through computerized lab analysis that not available for Borlaug's Nobel Prize research. Finally then, by the late 1990s Borlaug developed high-quality, double-protein seeds for corn to enhance the staple for the masses in much of the world. with much reduced use of fertilizers and chemicals.

India, in the meantime, had engaged beginning in 1991 in overuse of low-cost urea which has limited the yields in production, especially of rice, thus causing the Indian Green AgRevolution to wilt.[108] This is what Borlaug had feared would happen, and it had spurred him to advance his work on new seeds that would avoid the problem of stunted agricultural growth.

Behind India's worsening yields is the government's failure in agricultural policy, which has been trapped between (a) the need to boost food production while winning vote from farmers who constitute 70% of the electorate, and (b) the need to encourage

---

[108] This discussion of India agricultural problems follow the analysis by Geeta Anand, http://online.wsj.com/article/SB10 0014240527487036159045750529216127238844. html

India's fertilizer industry. The government resolved these competing goals by increasing its subsidy of urea to cover about half of its domestic production—this in spite of the fact that urea damages the land if over used.

When the government realized that the subsidy of urea was counterproductive, since 2009 it has sought to drop the existing subsidy system in favor of a new plan to allow urea's price to increase significantly, thus giving a disincentive for farmers to use many times the amount recommended by scientists, throwing off the chemistry of the soil. As Geeta Anand has noted, "like humans, plants need balanced diets to thrive. Too much urea oversaturates plants with nitrogen without replenishing [five key] nutrients that are vitally important, including phosphorus, potassium, sulfur, magnesium and calcium.[109] Under the new plan, the government will offer subsidies to fertilizer companies on the (especially on these five key nutrients), rather than the fertilizer products themselves. The idea is to provide incentives to the fertilizer industry and to farmers themselves to apply a better mix of nutrients. Until the use of urea is reduced, soil fertility will continue to decline causing evermore use of urea and evermore decline.

Mexico could learn from India's policy decision, and both countries need to shift to the Second Green AgRevolution by changing to proper use of GMO seeds. India has moved improperly and Mexico is only in 2009- 2010 experimenting with proper use, as advocated by Borlaug.

Meanwhile, Mexico, which has barely taken advantage of its own First Green Agricultural Revolution, has taken a different tack by improving the supply of food through its processing rather than its growing, and this tack has been led by RGB.

---

[109] Decentralized Globalization, Free Trade, Civil and Civic Society.2017

RGB has been able to refine the methods of making low-carbohydrate tortillas by adding fiber to the corn tortilla, thus reducing the high gross carbs to low net carbs to fight weight gain and diabetes. [110]The low- carb corn tortilla is vital for the poor who eat from 7 to 15 tortillas daily because they cannot afford to consume expensive meat, chicken, eggs, milk, or cheese needed for protein to offset the cheap high carb consumption.

Mission Carb Balance tortillas are low-carb tortillas that are high in dietary fiber. They have as few as 4 grams of net carbohydrates per tortilla, depending upon the type and size of the tortilla. The tortillas are available in whole wheat or white flour, and in soft taco, fajita, and burrito sizes.

In this process RGB has reduced dramatically the wastage of gas, electricity, water, food. (The industrial process of food too often results in a high wastage factor owing to inefficient processing.)

Borlaug again spent half his time in Mexico and half traveling the world seeking to expand the Second AgGreen Revolution, which is gaining a foothold in Africa as well as supporting CIMMyT affiliated research institutes such as the International Rice Research Institute in the Philippines, which has genetically modified seed to include vitamin A. (That vitamin has reduced the formerly high rate of blindness and eye afflictions in the Asia.)

RGB has expanded his processing plants from Mexico and the USA to Central America and beyond to Venezuela, England, China, Malaysia, Holland, Spain, and Italy.[111]

---

[110] See http://en.wikipedia.org/wiki/Gruma#Mission_Carb_Balance_tortillas

[111] See http://www.gruma.com/vEsp/NuestrasEmp/nuestras_empresas.asp

Both Borlaug and RGB have argued that the anti-GMOS movement fails to recognize that is easier to determine which new varieties of seeds carry allergies and how to remove them from the seeds. Such is not possible quickly and easily in the wholesale process of cross-breeding plant seeds—the method preferred by the anti-GMO groups.

Both Borlaug and RGB are concerned for the problem of feeding the world, the population of which is scheduled to grow exponentially (non-linearly) from 6.8 billion now to 18 billion by 2050. (See : **Decentralized Globalization, Free Trade, Civil and Civic Society.**) Also, New York Times Headline, September 13, 2008 By JUSTINGILLIS:www.nytimes.com/2009/09/14/business/energy-environment/14borlaug.html. Norman E. Borlaug, "the plant scientist who did more than anyone else in the 20th century to teach the world to feed itself and whose work was credited with saving hundreds of millions of lives, died [yesterday]. Dr. Borlaug's advances in plant breeding led to spectacular success in increasing food production in Latin America and Asia and brought him international acclaim. In 1970, he was awarded the Nobel Peace Prize."

He was widely described as the father of the broad agricultural movement called the Green Revolution, had a far-reaching impact on the lives of millions of people in developing countries. His breeding of high-yielding crop varieties helped to avert mass famines that were widely predicted in the 1960s, altering the course of history.

Largely because of his work, countries that had been food deficient, like Mexico and India, became self-sufficient in producing cereal grains.

"More than any other single person of this age, he has helped provide bread for a hungry world," the Nobel committee said in presenting him with the Peace Prize. "We have made this choice in the hope that providing bread will also give the world peace."

The day the award was announced, Dr. Borlaug, vigorous and slender at 56, was working in a wheat field outside Mexico City when his wife, Margaret, drove up to tell him the news. "Someone's pulling your leg," he replied, according to one of his biographers, Leon Hesser.

[Assured that the Nobel Award was true], Borlaug kept on working, saying he would celebrate later.

Criticism of Techniques

The Green Revolution eventually came under attack from environmental and social critics who said it had created more difficulties than it had solved. Dr. Borlaug responded that the real problem was not his agricultural techniques, but the runaway population growth that had made them necessary.

"If the world population continues to increase at the same rate, we will destroy the species," he declared.

FIGURE 8

Norman Borlaug, who helped teach the world to feed itself

Borlaug's concern about population growth is based on cancellations shown here in Figures 9 and 10. The problem is that the bigger the population becomes, the faster that it grows absolutely.

FIGURE 9

Two Alternative Methods of Making World Population Projections, 1955-2050

1. Arithmetic Model (Lineal), projection based on past data of "small" numbers of persons in the world which increase at past rate of increase

   Vs.

2. Geometric Model (Non-Linear), based on exponential growth rate where the larger the quantity gets, the faster it grows http:// en.wikipedia.org/wiki/Exponential_growth

Year	Arithmetical	Geometric
1955	2 779 968 031	2 819 942 263
1961	3 080 461 502	3 173 845 393
1972	3 862 348 766	4 800 596 395
1987	5 022 989 632	7 261 136 853
2000	6 085 478 778	
2009	6,800 000 000	
2020	7 510 699 958	10 150 412 281
2040	8 623 136 543	15 053 431 758
2050	9 050 494 208	18 332 067 005

* Source: U.S. Bureau of the Census, International Data Base. Total for mid-2009 = 6.8 billion persons, according to http://www.census.gov/ipc/www/popclockworld.html

[FLASH BACKWARD TO WHERE WE LEFT OFF IN THE ZEDILLO PRESIDENCY]

In the meantime, c faced the problem of one-party democracy in Mexico and its control by the Official Party, which too often had been authoritarian in nature (as from 1964 to 1982).

Zedillo's greatest accomplishment, in my view, was to work with opposition leader Porfirio Muñoz-Ledo (PML) to change the way in which Mexico voting takes place.[112] PML convinced Zedillo to implement removal of the PRI-Gobierno from its control over the corrupt IFE (Fed- eral Electoral System), the new IFE implicitly paving the way for defeat of the PRI's presidential candidate in 2000. (Salinas had reformed the Instituto Federal Electoral in 1994 to give majority control of IFE's General Council to six non-partisan "citizen counselors" elected by a two thirds vote in the Chamber of Deputies.[113])

Too, in 1996 Zedillo ceded Presidential authority to govern the Distrito Federal (D.F. or Federal District which is also called Mexico City) [114] to the new electoral system that allowed citizens to vote for their Jefe de Gobi- erno (also called by some "Regente" or "Mayor")

---

[112] PML did his doctoral studies the University of Toulouse, France, but did not complete his dissertation owing to his becoming involved in the LEA government.

[113] For a list of important legal reforms between 1982 and 2006, see K. Larry Storrs, http://assets.opencrs.com/rpts/RS22368_20060126.pD.F.

[114] http://es.wikipedia.org/wiki/Historia_del_Distrito_Federal_ (México)#Elementos_ del_gobierno_del_Distrito_Federal

and their own legislative assembly (Asamblea Legislativa). As a result of the first voting, the PRD won control of the D.F, which is virtually (if not legally) Mexico's 32nd state. Indeed the D.F. is the most populous "state" in Mexico and the most important in terms of politics and economics. The new mayor was Ing.[115]

Cuauhtémoc Cárdenas Solorzano (CCS, son of former President Lázaro Cárdenas), who had implicitly "won" but explicitly "lost" the presidential election of 1988, and who had clearly lost the 1994 presidential election.) [FLASH FORWARD: in 2000, CCS would fade to third place in the presidential contest.]

Since 1997, the PRD has controlled the Federal District (Distrito Federal, or D.F.), which is actually a virtual state not headed by a governor but by a Jefe de Gobierno (formerly called Regente or Head of the "Department of the D.F." and, more recently, Mayor). [116] The states fear that if the D.F. were to become a full-fledged state that its power (already huge as the capital city of the country) would overwhelm all legislative activities and budget resources at the expense of the other 31 states. Given this political struggle, the city is colloquially known as "Chilangolandia" after the locals' nickname chilangos, which is used either as a pejorative term by people living outside Mexico City or as a proud adjective by Mexico City's dwellers.

---

[115] "Ing." is he abbreviation for Ingeniero ("Engineer" in English); CCS had done graduate studies and internships in civil engineering in Europe.) In Mexico, the elite must have a title, especially and even on the left to prove that they are "somebody important."

[116] The D.F. itself is divided into 16 "Delegaciones," each of which has had since 1997 its own Jefe de Gobierno de la Delagación —the head was formerly named by the Jefe de Gobierno of the D.F.). For this 2007 update on the D.F., and for aspects of its history, see http://en.wikipedia.org/wiki/Mexico_City#Federal_District

The question remains: when will Mexico City, now a de facto state government, gain the full de jure powers of the other Mexican states?— the D.F. has sent Senators and Deputies to the National Congress going back to the origins of the PNR; and since 1997 the D.F.'s "Legislative Assembly" (which has succeeded the previous "Assembly" with appointed members) has 66 "representatives" who are elected by popular vote to this unicameral body. In effect, the D.F. Assembly is the most important elected body in Mexico after the National Congress. The D.F. has in the past set the trend for the nation as a whole, but….

[FLASH FORWARD:
Against the wishes of President Calderón, the Catholic Church, and many conservative states such as Guanajuato:

i. In 2007, the D.F approved same-sex unions between two persons and with right to adopt children—it was the second federal entity in the country to do so after the state of Coahuila); and
ii. In the D.F. became the first to allow conjugal visits for homo- sexual prisoners.
iii. In April 2007, the Legislative Assembly became the first federal entity to expand abortion in Mexico (beyond cases of rape and economic reasons) to permit it regardless of the reason should the mother request it before the twelfth week of pregnancy— in the backlash by the end of 2009, 17 states have defined life as beginning at conception, effectively defining abortion as murder.
iv. In December 2009, the Federal District became the first city in Latin America, and one of very few in the world, to legalize same- sex marriage.]

Issues of abortion and same-sex marriage were not the issues that Zedillo faced in 1997, but rather the mid-presidential term elections of 1997, in which the PRI loses control of the D.F. as well as loses its majority in the Chamber of Deputies and its two-thirds majority in the Senate. The elections demonstrated that the opposition would have a new role in Mexico.

Indeed, in 1997 opposition parties PRD and PAN win a majority in the Chamber of Deputies (when and if they held together), the PRD and PAN hold 5 of 32 governorships, [117] including the D.F., discussed above

In 2000 the PRI lost the presidential election, a result foreordained by the independent status of the new IFE and the fact that Porfirio Muñoz-Ledo (PML had left the PRD to run as the PARM candidate) shifted his support to Fox. PML was the first major leader to shift his support—important because he abandoned his own campaign.

Also important in the Fox win was the unpopularity of the PRI candidate Francisco Labastida, who stated during his campaign that he would not legalize the many thousands of "autos chocolate," that is "used cars and pickup trucks smuggled into Mexico" to meet the needs of the poor. (The popular sector cannot afford to buy new Mexican car or even pay for used autos sold in Mexico at higher prices and on which one pays high taxes.)

Also, by 2000 much of the Mexican population had seen the video of the 1995 massacre of peaceful peasants by police at Aguas Blancas outside of Acapulco,[118] planned and carried out at the orders of the PRI governor, forcefully reminding Mexico of the 71 years of PRI impunity.

---

[117] See K. Larry Storrs.

[118] See http://en.wikipedia.org/wiki/Aguas_Blancas_massacre

Ironically, some authors see the end of the Revolution as having occurred in 2000. Indeed Donald Hodges and Ross Gandy implicitly accept Fuente's view that the end came with "stages of death" but do not see the stages ending in 1959 (the Fuentes date for final systemic breakdown), but rather they present the stages as being 1968, 1982, and 2000—the last marking final death of the Revolution . See their book Mexico: The End of the Revolution.[119] If only issues were so clear (as Hodges and Gandy argue implicitly) about Mexico having had only one Revolution....

13c. Active-Statist Revolution Under President Vicente Fox (2000- 2006), who follows Salinas model of Active States, even while speaking in Anti-State terms Fox defeated the one-party system but not its basis in bureaucracies; and the PRI, which continues to govern in more than half of the 32 states Under Fox the population increases from 99 million in 2000 to 112 million in 2010.

> Although the PRI fell from presidential power in 2000, in early 2008 the PRI was still the second most important power in the nation's Senate, with 26% (and third power in the National Chamber of Deputies with 21%)—thus it is still the key player to provide a "coalition" to govern the country.[120]
>
> Most importantly, since 2008 the PRI still controls more than 56% of Mexico's 32 state governorships, 63% of the 32 state congresses, and 37% of Mexico's municipal governments. Although the PRD controls Mexico City proper, over half of Greater Mexico City's 20 million persons

---

[119] See http://books.google.com/books?id=Fk9J W140bJ8C&printsec=frontcover

[120] Dr. Fernando González Reynoso (Professor of Sociology, Universidad Autónoma de Baja California), presentation to my Graduate Seminar at UCLA, December 5, 2007.

live under a PRI governor.[121] Of the Mexican population, 57% live under PRI governors.[122]

Since the PRI lost the presidency in 2000 to the PANista Vicente Fox (MBA and former President of Coca-Cola de México), it has become the Former Official Party or PRI/FOP, which continues to play a major role in Mexican politics.

Fox's problem from the outset of taking office was that he had won his position with only 43% of the vote and his party was one of three in the Congress, each not able to pass legislation without gaining a temporary alliance with the other. The main alliance that emerged for most votes was PAN/PRI, but that was always tenuous.

As President of Mexico (2000-2006), one of Fox's greatest accomplishments was to have defeated the PRI and take the presidency from the Official Party in 2000—he himself sees Zedillo's greatest presidential success as having established an independent Federal Electoral Commission (IFE) and for having announced on election night that the IFE results had made Fox President of Mexico.

Another of his accomplishments was to establish in 2002 a Freedom of Information Act to provide the transparency necessary for civic groups to hold the government accountable for its actions.[123] Fox also indicted LEA for genocide in the massacres of "leftists" in

---

[121] On Greater Mexico City, see http://en.wikipedia.org/wiki/Greater_Mexico_City# Demographics

[122] PRI Governor Gov. Mario Marín of Puebla was tape recorded by his wife in 2005 as he planned how to kidnap Lydia Cacho, a reporter investigating child prostitution and sexual abuse of young girls. See Cacho, *Los Demonios del Eden*, http://graficos. eluniversal.com.mx/a/audios/audios.htm

[123] See: Kate Doyle, http://www.gwu.edu/~nsarchiv/NSAEBB/NSAEBB68/

1968 (when he was Minister of Gobernación) and 1971 (during his Presidency.) LEA spent several years under house arrest before winning his appeal that the statute of limitations had expired. The very indictment of a former President, however, doomed LEA to live under self-imposed "house arrest" because for him to be seen in public meant humiliation by citizens who revile him.

In 2004 Fox established Seguro Popular (System of Popular Health Insurance). About this plan and its implementation, Julio Frenk, Minister of Health of Mexico, who developed the country's 6-year project to expand the healthcare system spoke positively on September 7, 2006: [124]

"This initiative was introduced to improve universal access to health insurance, medicines, and heath care and reduce the numbers living in poverty. In 2000, analysis of national data revealed that many Mexican families suffered catastrophic expenditure or were forced below the poverty line by the cost of health care and medicines. This was directly related to health insurance being limited to salaried employees in private firms or in public-sector institutions. To address this problem the Seguro Popular scheme [has] made it possible for [millions of] Mexicans to access publicly subsidized health insurance.

"Seguro Popular (and its associated Fund for Protection against Cata- strophic Expenses) includes a specific package of benefits enabling people to access more than 250 health promotion and disease prevention measures, including outpatient care and hospital care for the basic specialties, antiretroviral therapy, intensive care for newborns, cancer care, and haemodialysis. By the end of this year Seguro Popular will have enrolled the [planned] 22 million people," and is making an attempt to achieve universal coverage by 2011, unfortunately without enough doctors, hospitals, medicines,

---

[124] Quoted from http://www.news-medical.net/?id=19986

and x-rays to service this huge group. In 2010, Seguro Popular is adding enrollments of families in Mexico through payments by workers to Seguro Social at Mexican Consulates, [125]thus raising again the number of persons covered b the Mexican health system.

The real result, then, is not so positive. Theoretically the clinics and hospitals of the Mexican Social Security System and the Ministry of Public Health are supposed to open their door to the uninsured, but given the fact that they are already overwhelmed by the insured population which has paid premiums it is hard to find space and time for a new population that has not paid for health coverage. Indeed, the idea of offering free healthcare has led to the question: Is it not a counter-incentive for persons to pay premiums? Further, although the population has a right to free medicines and x-rays, the Mexican health systems are frequently out of stock of what is needed most, and persons must purchase their own Rx or x-ray film to be used by the clinic or hospital. The middle class which pays into the Social Security System tries not to use it, unless a friend who is a physician who works there can cut through the red-tape and waiting times. Yet for the poor (the so-called "popular sector"), Seguro Popular is better than nothing.

On the front of "land reform," Fox had the courage to realize that further distribution of land into Ejidos was counter-productive and should not be required. Thus, in 2002 he changed the land reform regulatory law to make Ejidal distributions as optional and only for exceptional reasons.

At the behest of PROFMEX, Fox brought to Mexico Hernando de Soto, the Peruvian expert in sorting out land titles in countries around the world. But de Soto found that over half Mexico's land

---

[125] See www.impre.com/noticias/2010/1/13/seguro-popular-es-otra-opcion-168221-1. html www.segupopular.salud.gob.mx/contenidos/seguro_popular/seguro_popular.html

titles are so tangled in ownership claims that he could not help expedite titles so that "owners" could pledge their property as collateral to obtain a loan.

Fox has stated that in his view of six years as President that he made other major gains,[126] having achieved (in addition to the other positive factors given above) more than:

> 25 millones de mexicanos en situación de pobreza reciben los apoyos del Programa Oportunidades.
> 6 millones de niñas, niños y jóvenes cuentan con una beca para continuar sus estudios.
> 3 millones de familias cumplieron el sueño de tener una vivi- enda propia."

Things did not always go as well for Fox as he wanted. He inherited from Zedillo a real foreign debt total of US$ 181 billion, which he reduced to US$ 133 billion. The PAN was proud of this achievement, which its leaders saw as taking a realistically conservative approach to the role of the federal government, thus continuing its long attempt to break the power of Corporativism and its attempt to hold on to Statist power.

Given the failure of PEMEx to find and develop new reserves, Fox toyed with the idea of inviting foreign capital with the cash reserves and technology for deep-water drilling in the Gulf, which are beyond Mexico's reach, but he gave up when the PEMEx sindicatos threatened to strike and blow up production facilities. The good news, however, was that Fox inherited a country of diverse exports—in 1980 oil exports accounted for 62% of total exports; by 2000 it was only 7%,127[127] the word "only" can also

---

[126] See: http://fox.presidencia.gob.mx/vicentefox/

[127] See http://en.wikipedia.org/wiki/Economy_of_Mexico

be used ironically to reflect the corruption of PEMEx and theft of millions of oil daily to sell it to the private sector.

But Fox's critics as slow learner in the battle to circumvent the Corporativist bureaucracy, which prevented him from making expenditure spending authorized funds.

To avoid intrigue in Mexico, Fox spent a huge amount of time traveling the world,[128] where he felt "safe" from internal criticism in Mexico. Even there, Fox often got into trouble when he revealed his low level of cul- tural literacy and had to defend himself for not knowing the name of the world famous Argentine author Jorge Luis Borges: "Well, they criticized me because I said 'José Luis Borgues,'" Fox said; "but surely, anyone can make a bilingual slip of the tongue".129[129] Yet for many he seemed much more literate than his fellow president and fellow holder of an MBA to the north—Bush II, who also pretended to be a cowboy. In another revealing slip, Fox called his friend

Bush II a "Windshield Cowboy" because he seemed to be afraid of horses while visiting the Fox ranch in Mexico and preferred to ride the range in a jeep.

In the meantime, Fox was ridiculed for making his own cowboy boots into his trade-mark symbol of machismo, and he made them the official gift to the world leaders who he visited. But his usage

---

[128] Fox's memoirs are written in the "I" form (but are co-authored by Rob Allyn). They focus on his world travels and people he has come to know. The memoirs contain few insights hidden in much insignificant gossip (perhaps the way he saw the world: *Revolution of hope: the life, faith, and dreams of a Mexican president* (New York: Viking, 2007); Edition in Spanish: *La Revolución de la Esperanza: La vida, los anhelos y los suenos de un presidente.*

[129] See www.barcelonametropolis.cat/en/page.asp?id=22& ui=89&prevNode=35&tagId=Sergi%20Doria

of that symbol backfired: boots are not made for riding horseback, not walking. Fox damaged his spine from wearing them constantly, and in March 2003 had to undergo back surgery—from which he has never fully recovered. Although he stopped wearing boots, back pain did not make his difficult presidency any easier.

The surgery raised a serious issue, which remains unresolved: [130]Because Mexico's constitution does not spell out who is in charge when the Mexican president cannot govern, the question arose about the need to create the position of vice president in Mexico.

Presidential transition itself was difficult in 2006, but resolved. 13d Felipe Calderón (2006-2012) implicity rules for Active-State Policy, even though he campaigned in Anti-State terms During the 4 years from 2007-2010, the population increased from 106 million to 112 million, growth abetted by the U.S. closure of its border with Mexico, deportation from the USA of Mexicans working without U.S. documents or found guilty of even minor crimes, and the voluntarary return to Mexico by those who lost jobs during Depression II in the USA.

Calderón of the PAN won the presidency July 2, 2006, and took office December 1, after a bitterly disputed partial electoral recount.

It was the appropriate time for PAN was able to recall how long it had sought to prevent the rise of Statism since the Party's founding in 1939. Calderón, who campaigned in Anti-State terms converted to Active State actions when he took office.

Calderón "realized" that the vision of Mexico's accumulated Grandes Problemas Nacionales (which had last been updated and

---

[130] See http://airwolf.lmtonline.com/news/archive/031303/pagea10.pdf.

attacked with verve under Salinas's Active State Policy) needed to be revised and attacked anew.

Calderón, then, without announcing a Plan that would bring down the wrath perhaps all of the major interest groups in Mexico, began to articulate the basis for reviving strong Active State Policy not seen since the Salinas 12-years in power. As we see, many elements have been added to his Plan as he has maneuvered his way through the Mexican political scene, as we see below.

Fortunately for Calderon, by the time he took office, two protest groups which once seemed to threaten the power of Mexico government had faded into the background, with only a sputter in 2007.

The Peoples' Revolutionary Party (ERP, Ejército Revolucionario del Pueblo) emerges now and then from its hideouts in the mountains of Guerrero and Oaxaca (where it was founded in 1996) to apply the lessons learned by guerrillas around the world. (The ERP was among those who watched the U.S. face problems in the bombing of oil pipelines in Iraq). More than 10 major bombings in Mexico in 2007 disrupted oil and gas supplies and stopped industrial production while pipelines are repaired.

But then suddenly the bombing of the oil pipelines stopped— leading many observes to question whether the bombs were placed by the ERP,[131] or by dissidents in the PEMEx Sindicato, who may have been warding the government against allowing foreign private capital to become involved in the extraction of oil. (Too, someone with exact knowledge about the oil pipeline system had

---

[131] In recent communiqués, the ERP mainly protests about disappearance of members at the hands of authorities, threatening action unless the disappeared are make to reappear.

to have set the bombs, and that would need guidance from persons inside PEMEx.)

Subcomandante Marcos had won implicit recognition as a political group (not a guerrilla group) when in 2001 President Fox invited the EzLN to march to Mexico City and make Marcos's case in Congress. The presentation resulted in the release of most EzLN prisoners and permitted them to move freely about Mexico. Indeed in 2006, Marcos conducted his "Other Campaign" (as Comandante Zero) against presidential candidates Calderón and AMLO. In the end, he endorsed AMLO, but too late to make a difference. Marcos still calls for an "Indigenous Nation" within the Mexican Nation. But after the presidential electoral recount, which Marcos had predicted would never take place, (let alone a real election), he lost relevance.

In terms of the economy, Real GDP growth rates under the PAN declined dramatically, as they had under the PRI. From 1981 through 2000, the PRI's yearly average had fallen to 2.4%. ("Real GDP" removes the effect of inflation from the data, which otherwise understates past change and overstates current change.) Mexico's low GDP growth was influenced by the 2001 attack on the USA 9/11.

The PAN's average Real GDP growth rate from 2001 through 2006 was not the 7.5% promised, but also only 2.4% (see Figure 11), in spite of increasing remittances from Mexican workers in the USA (US$ 26 billion in 2006) and rising world oil prices (which reached US$ 148 per barrel in July 2007 (vs. US$ 20 in 2000). Mexico's blend of petroleum sells for 10-20% less than U.S. West Texas Intermediate, which is the world bench-mark price that had reached only US$ 100 per barrel in 2007. In 2009 the U.S. price collapsed to the $50 per bbl. range, gravely affecting Mexico's income from oil exports. During the transition from 2009 to 2010, oil has hovered near $80, with upward tendency.

The Real GDP of Mexico's growth rate reached 5.2% in 2006 (thus winning presidential votes for Calderón), but has subsequently fell back to an average of 2.3% during Calderón's first two years—2007 and 2008.[132] (See Figure 11, for graphic views.)

---

[132] See http://www.tradingeconomics.com/Economics/ GDP-Growth.aspx?Symbol= MXN

FIGURE 11

Mex GDP

Mexico/Gross domestic product (2008) **1.11 trillion USD (2008)** **Canada** 1.549 trillion USD (2008) **Brazil** 1.696 trillion USD (2008) **RELATED STATISTICS**	
GDP per capita	10,016.57 USD (2008)
Population	110.8 million (2008)
GDP growth rate	1.1% annual change (2008)

FIGURE 12

World GDP Collapse, 2008-2009, Recovery for the Rich in 2010 ("Economic and Financial Indicators, Economist, December 9 2010)

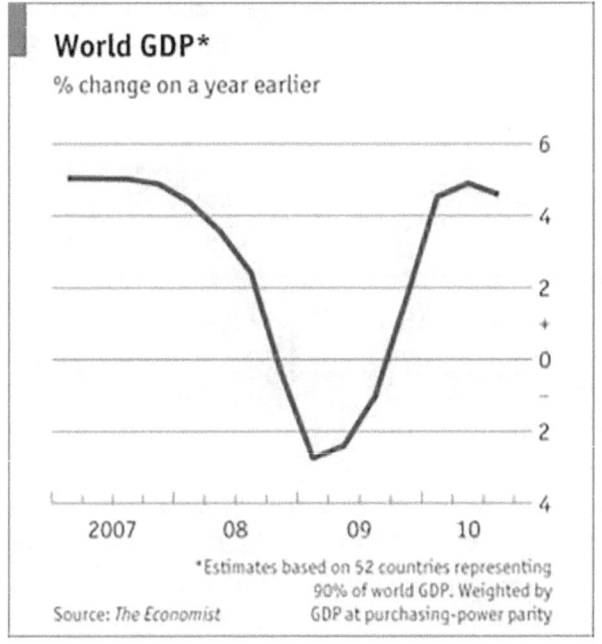

In 2009, GDP suffered the worst collapse of any major country in the world, falling 7.1%, exceeding even the fall of the Russian and Hungar- ian GDPs (-7.0%).[133]

---

[133] "Economic and Financial Indicators," The Economist, Jan. 9, 2009.

13d.1 Calderón Faces López-Obrador (AMLO), Who Wants Anarchy to Restore Statist Revolution

Andrés Manuel López-Obrador (who ran the "Main Campaign" against Calderón in the Presidential Election of 2006) has proclaimed himself to be the "Legitimate President" (2006-2012), and he still promises to lay the basis for shifting Mexico back to Statism. His foreign allies do not include the USA but, Chávez in Venezuela, the Kirchners in Argentina, Evo Morales in Bolivia, Rafael Correa in Ecuador, Lula in Brazil, and what is left of Fidel Castro in Cuba. He "prohibited" members of the PRD, including the Mayor of Mexico City, to have any relations with the Calderón Administration, although the Mayor's chief assistants were allowed to negotiate in order to keep federal subsidies flowing to the largest city in Mexico.

AMLO considered the PRD to be "His" Party of the Democratic Revolution (PRD) which he "owned" as "Jefe de Jefes" when the party base decided that his refusal to negotiate with Calderón and/or cooperate with the Calderón government was making the PRD irrelevant. The goal in 2009 then became how to sideline AMLO and give the PRD authority to work constructively with the government.

In seeking prevent the privatizing of PEMEx or the Mexican Electricity Industry, AMLO has refused to consider even doing so in part, even with the State maintaining majority control. Indeed, AMLO seeks to end PEMEx from making service contracts—ironically, except for Coca- Cola to provide beverages for PEMEx workers. The purpose of service contracts, e.g., is to permit PEMEx to hire deep-water drilling expertise from abroad—expertise which PEMEx lacks.

In late 2008, AMLO lost his bid to continue his control of the PRD when Jesús "Chucho" Ortega defeated AMLO's candidate to become the new President of PRD. Jesús (and his chief operator Jesús Zambrano) who deem themselves to be "Los Chuchos") now are seeking to portray the PRD as the "Renewed PRD". With AMLO displaced by 2009, he is withdrawing from the PRD.

In short, Chucho (the nickname of all those named "Jesus) won the PRD presidency by basing his campaign to recognize Calderón as President and work with the PRD (and PRI) to solve Mexico's problems, thus defeating AMLO's anarchical policies.[134]

In the meantime the two PRD founders Porfirio M uñoz Ledo and Cuauhtémoc Cárdenas (who have long been enemies) have taken different positions: the former supporting AMLO, the latter opposing him and suggesting that he himself (Cuauhtémoc) should again be candidate for President of Mexico.

The Ebrard W ing of the PRD:[135] Marcelo Ebrard (currently "Mayor" of Mexico City and Jefe de Gobierno of Mexico's Federal District that includes Mexico City) must position himself as a rationale, independent political leader. Ebrard had followed AMLO's orders not to meet personally with any officials of the Calderón government.

Ebrard's critics argue that he governs Mexico City through the use of kommissars (spies who politicize all activities as potential conspiracies, as in the old USSR). His supporters include Manuel Camacho-Solís, who during the Salinas era of the PRI served as Mayor of the D.F., 1988- 1993. Critics of Camacho claim that he

---

[134] See John Ross, "The Demise of the PRD," http:// www.counterpunch.org/ ross05172008.html

[135] See www.angelfire.com/tn/tiempos/politica/texto314.html

is intent on reviving the "Old Authoritarian PRI Style," but this statement seems exaggerated.

13d.2 Narcotraficantes (Drug Traffickers) Seek Anarchy to Neutralize Police & Military. Gerardo García Luna helps them.

Narcotraficantes k ill Mexican police and s oldiers to disrupt the police power of the government, which seeks to put the drug dealers out of business. The Narcotraficantes are better paid and have better communication than the police and army. They certainly have better weapons (including shoulder-fired missiles) than the police and often outgun even most military units. They pay enormous bribes to avoid scrutiny by government internal security "forces." If they successfully create anarchy by paralyzing the role of police and army, they win the right to freely traffic in drugs— they do not want to try to govern Mexico.

Perhaps to show personal strength just days after being sworn into office December 1 2006 (with a bare winning margin of only .58% of the vote), Calderón declared 10 days later that he was sending Federal troops to stop the drug violence in his home state of Michoacán. This act would turn into the War on Drug Cartels throughout Mexico.

But even more important than any political weakness for Calderón decision to take on the Drug Cartels is the fact that Calderón had the personal courage to realize that the Federal government could no longer ignore the increasingly violent Narcotraficantes who decade by decade since the 1980s had become evermore murderous as they "challenged" the Mexican State. Thus, in his first month in office Calderón sent an initial 6,500 troops to quash a rash of execution-style killings between two rival drug gangs in Michoácan.[136] Since 2006, the number of troops have risen as they spread throughout Mexico to surpass 45,000 in the struggle against the Drug Cartels.

Also, in 2006 Calderón undertook the first of many campaigns to clean up police corruption in Mexico when his public security minister Genaro García-Luna removed 284 federal police commissioners on corruption charges and replaced them with a hand-selected group of officers who successfully arrested several drug kingpins. The gangs have responded with what seems to be an endless stream of violence—more than 16,000 people have been killed in drug-related crimes during the last three years December 2006 to December 2009, the vast majority being narcotraficantes but also including innocents caught in the cross- fire a well as over 150 police and troops.

The total killed persons, about whom are known, the total rose to 32,000 for the period 2006-2010 is shown yearly in Figure 14 .

But let us not forget the history dating back to the 1985 murder of DEA agent Enrique Camarena, when Mexico and the USA became fully aware of the danger posed by Narcotraficantes—see 13a, above.

El Chapo was captured in 1993 but escaped prison in 1995 on the eve of his extradition to the USA—as of the end of 2010 he has still at large.

---

[136] **For two analyses of what can only be called the failed U.S. War on Drugs and U.S. historical context of many muddled matters in helping to resolve Mexican issues to combat the narcotraficantes**, see. e.g., Claire Sudda and Philip Caputo. Sudda, ["Mexico's] War on Drugs," March 25, 2009, is at www.time.com/time/ worldarticle/0,8599,1887488,00.html and Caputo on "**The Fall of Mexico**", *Atlantic Magazine*, Dec. 2009 is at www.theatlantic.com/doc/200912/mexico-drugs

In 2008, El Chapo Guzman was listed at 701 on the Forbes' list of richest people in the world with an estimated net worth of $2 billion, which infuriated Mexican authorities who saw his inclusion on the list as an insult to the civilized world. The head of Mexican Security Gerard Garcia Luna, had been the architect of the USA-Mexico drug wars. the leading figure behind Mexico's Calderon war on drugs. Known number of persons killed in Mexico's Drug War. 2006-2010* (May be Up to 56,000 or More in 2018.) He moved to Florida, in

> Miami
> 32,000 total* (including crossfire)**
> 486 Dec. 2006
> 2,477 in 2007 (including 300 in Juárez)
> 6,290 in 2008 (including 1,620 in Juárez)
> 7,724 in 2009 (including 2,660 in Ciudad Juárez***)
> 15,023 in 2010 (including 3,111 in Juárez; about 25% of the cities 1.4 million persons have fled. 56.000 dead in 2018

*This total since 2006 agrees with that of Mexican officials who dis- agree with the total of 30,200 given by Mexico's Attorney General Arturo Chávez (see PressTV, Jan. 3, 2011: http://www.presstv.ir/ detail/158388.html

Other sources claim that Chávez has a data base with 36,000 names of persons killed in the Drug Wars, see Gardenia Mendoza Aguilar, Dec. 17, 2010 http://www.impre.com/noticias/2010/12/17/son- 36-mil-muertos-por-la-narc-228638-1.html#commentsBlock

**Statistics on the loss of life are complicated in Mexico, thus there is no single list but rather many, depending on the focus of the compiler, whose lists include: Men and women murdered, human bones found but not identified and/or identifiable, persons killed in battles between drug cartels and/or with the military, persons killed by crossfire, persons killed in kidnappings and/or robberies, migrants killed, apparent suicides, children murdered by family and/or foe, women killed by "Satanic Cults," women factory work- ers who are missing and also missing and presumed dead, etc, In 2009 Ken Ellingwood articulated in his August 8 article for the Los Angeles Times the sudden rise of missing women who are students leaving behind stable middle-and working-class families—see www.latimes.com/news/nationworld/world/la-fg-juarez-missing9- 2009aug09,0,4357807.story

***The Ciudad Juárez total includes 194 cases of "femicide" in 2009 and total of 750 women since 1993—the latter figure is given in the Inter-American Court of Human Rights Report quoted in http:// www.elpasotimes.com/ci_13981319

Femicide is the mass murder of women simply because they are women. It is the term that has been coined in response to the hundreds of women murdered and missing on the U.S.-Mexico border in the city of Juarez, just across the border from El Paso, Texas.

Some lists show "only" 350 women missing/dead from 1993-2009, others give figures in the 450 range. The high is 750.

Source: Drawn from: http://en.wikipedia.org/wiki/Mexican_Drug_ War as well as from the always excellent reportage by Gardenia Mendoza-Aguilar, www.impre.com/laopinion/noticias/2009/12/28/ mas-barbaros-los-actos-de-los—165786-1.html and Ioan Grillo, "Mexico's Cocaine Capital." Time. August 14, 2008, www.time.com/ time/magazine/article/0,9171,1832854,00.html See also: http://www.presstv.ir/detail/158388.html (Jan. 3, 2011)

In November 2009, Forbes Magazine ranked Joaquín Guzmán as the 41st of 67 most powerful people in the world, angering American and Mexican officials.

During the early 2000s improvements in illegal flights detection prompted El Chapo to diversify transportation methods and routes. Guzmán is well known for his use of sophisticated tunnels to smuggle cocaine from Mexico into the United States in the early 1990s. In 1993 a 7.3 ton shipment of his cocaine, concealed in cans of chile peppers and destined for the United States, was seized in Baja California..[137]

Presidents Bush and Calderón agreed, in 2007,138[138] to the Mérida Initiative for eventually providing $1.6 billion to Mexico and other countries over three years to help combat drug smuggling and violence. Of the $1.1 billion allocated to Mexico (via the transfer of military equipment and the training of police, prosecutors, and judges—not by direct transfer of funds), the end of 2009 saw only $83 million (7%) worth of goods and service had been received by Mexico and that required a a's Secretary of State, Hillary Clinton, to personally cut through the U.S. bureaucracy to help Mexican begin to mount a greater operations level, which had stalled under Bush in 2007 and 2008 and under Obama in 2009.[139]

By late 2009 and early 2010, however, the U.S. Electronic Surveillance, pay- ments to informants, and analysis of "life styles"

---

[137] See http://en.wikipedia.org/wiki/Joaqu%C3%ADn_Guzm%C3%A1n_Loera

[138] See http://en.wikipedia.org/wiki/Mérida_Initiative

[139] On the "failure" of Mérida initiative to move quickly, see Gardenia Mendoza- Aguilar, www.impre.com/laopinion/noticias/2009/12/28/mas-barbaros-los-actos-de- los—165786-1.html

has guided Mexican forces to such key narcotraficantes as Arturo Beltrán Leyva (killed in a December 2009 shootout in Cuernavaca and his brother Carlos arrested in Culiacán within days) and El Teo Simentel (arrested in La Paz, Baja California, January 2010).

In spite of the lack of U.S. "virtual funds" promised to help Mexico, the Calderón government announced the "2009 scorecard" with some positive results in the Mexico Drug War. Figure 16 gives the scorecard. (Virtual support is an "insult" to the Mexican government because the U.S. Congress has mandated that U.S. payments be made directly to the provider of services and not through the Mexican government. This insult has been partially "compensated" by the U.S. providing electronic tracking support to locate capos.)

Low pay military is a problem for Mexico because the Narcotraficantes offer much, much more in pay and benefits—see Figure 15

FIGURE 15

Monthly Earnings in Mexico Narco Wars (US$)

Army Soldier	Narco Warrior (Estimated)	"Sicario" Common Hit-Man
2006 $ 360		
2010 $ 640	US$ 10K AK-47, SUV, "chain-saw", cell phone, home for family znd top quality medical plan	US$ 50 per killing by a Sicario
2011 $ 720 (plan) now	Bonuses are set in increase	Some Sicarios may claim to be "underpaid" in light of the arrest of an American 12-year-old* was paid $200 weekly** in 2010 (but that salary included torture and dismemberment)

*For news and video of "El Ponchis", see http://www.borderlandbeat.com/2010/11/ruthless-sicario-is-only-12-years-old.html

> ** For an interview with "El Ponchis," see http://www.immortaltechnique. co.uk/Thread-El-Ponchis-14-YEAR-OLD-NARC-THAT-SLIT-THROATS- CONFESSES

FIGURE 16

Calderón's Positive and Negative Drug War Scorecard, 2009 (If you need a translation, see the Course Website)

Noticias positivas:
+ Presuntos narcotraficantes detenidos 11 mil 297
+ Principales capos caídos:
"El Teo" Teodoro García-Simentel,* jefe de jefes en Tijuana, 1-12- 2010, fundador de la "narcoguerra sin reglas y sin piedad" en abril de 2008
Arturo Beltrán-Leyva, ex jefe del cartel de Sinaloa, killed 12-15-2009
Vicente Carrillo-Leyva, hijo del extinto Amado Carrillo Fuentes, fundador del cartel de Juárez;
Vicente zambada-niebla, alias El Vicentillo, hijo de
Ismael 'El Mayo' zambada, uno de los jefes del cartel de Sinaloa.
+ Funcionarios involucrados con el narcotráfico: 362; incluyendo 54 militares

+ Decomiso de cocaína 12 toneladas
+ Decomiso de vehículos 5,882
+ Decomiso de armas 15 mil
+ Erradicación de marihuana y amapola 17,563 hectáreas

Noticias negativas:

- Ejecutados por los narcotraficantes (and/or killed in crossfire): 7,500
- Día más violento: 17 de diciembre con 64 muertos

*"El Teo, quien había sido reclutado en 1995 por Ramón Arellano- Félix, en abril de 2008 rompió con el cártel de Tijuana supuestamente al mando de Fernando Sánchez-Arellano 'El Ingeniero' para dar inicio a la 'narcoguerra' [sin reglas, sin piedad]. "Es cuando toma el control de la estructura del crimen y narcotráfico en Baja California.... Para mantener el financiamiento de su estructura operativa El Teo recurría al secuestro de empresarios y comerciantes en sus principales zonas de operación, Ensenada Rosarito, Tijuana y Tecate".

"En esa narcoguerra empiezan a surgir decapitados, colgados y cadá- veres disueltos en ácido. Los 'narcomensajes' dan cuenta de los moti- vos de cada uno de los cuerpos que se localizaban regados en la ciudad [en la batalla]: El Teo vs. El Ingeniero,...

"El Teo se le vincula con la mayoría de las ejecuciones de policías municipales, estatales y federales, así como de funcionarios públicos, como el de Rogelio Sánchez-Jiménez, empleado del gobierno del estado, a quien encontraron desnudo y con huellas de tortura, col- gado de un puente en Tijuana el 8 de octubre de 2009.

"Luego se incrementaron las amenazas en contra del procurador estatal Rommel Moreno, y del jefe de la policía local, Julián Leyzaola.

"En 2004, junto con su hermano Marco Antonio García-Simental, 'El Chris'; Efraín Pérez-Pasuengo, 'El Efra', y Jorge Aureliano-Félix, 'El Macumba', [El Teo se habiá integrada] a la estructura operacional del trasiego de droga a Estados Unidos," según Jorge

Morales-Aldama, www.impre.com/noticias/2010/1/13/ policia-mexicana-captura-a-el—168223-1.htm Source: Adapted from Gardenia Mendoza-Aguilar, "Más Bárbaros los actos de los Narcos," La Opinión, December 28, 2009 at www. impre.com/laopinion/noticias/2009/12/28/mas-barbaros-los-actos- de-los—165786-1.html

MAP 4

The Reach of Mexico's Drug Cartels, 2009

The State of Mexico's Drug Wars With Scott Stewart and Fred Burton

FIGURE 17

Mexican Drug Cartels and Their Capos—Living and Dead, 2009 Excluding Non-Functioning Cartels and New Possible Strong Cartels, e.g.

http://en.wikipedia.org/wiki/Los_Negros(Many Capos are Still Living, But in Prison: see Interactive Link: http://en.wikipedia.org/wiki/Timeline_of_the_Mexican_Drug_War

Name of Cartel	Number of Capos	Still living at the end of 2009
Beltran Leyva Cartel Sinaloa	6	3 but Carlos arrested in Culiacán 12-30-09 (14 days after "El Jefe" Arturo killed in Cuernavaca by Elite Mexican Navy Squad)*

La Familia Michocána	10	2, the Maximum Leader "El Más Loco" having been killed in late 2010, the Mexican Government announced this gang of Nar- cotraficantes now "disarticulated." But not before bloody battles in which the gang effectively sealed off for some days the state capital of Morelia.
Gulf Cartel	12	11 but one in U.S. prison (Garciá-Abrego) & one (Osiel Cárde- nas-Guillén) in Mexican insecure prison where he can still operate the Cartel, however, see "zetas," belowfor Alliance
Juárez Cartel	8	7 but the notorius Rafael Caro-Quintero Prison in Mexico, and Miguel Caro-Quintero is in U.S. prison
Sinaloa Cartel	8	8 but, e.g., Miguel Ángel Félix-Gal- lardo is in high security prison

*See www.google.com/hostednews/canadianpress/ article/ALeqM5j0n SLAq5dnPnRtwgckASlqhTgAeQ

**In addition to conducting activities along the border, the Zetas Cartel is active throughout the Gulf Coast region, in the Southern states of Tabasco, Yucatan, Quintana Roo, and Chiapas, and in the Pacific Coast states of Guerrero, Oaxaca, and Michoacán, as well as in Mexico City. At times it has operated in Ciudad Juárez in support of remnants of the old Carrillo Fuentes Cartel, and perhaps other groups who oppose the Caro-Quintero Cartel.

SOURCE: La Opinión; http://en.wikipedia.org/wiki/Timeline_ of_the_ Mexican_Drug_War & http://en.wikipedia.org/wiki/Los_ Zetas as well as http://treas.gov/press/releases/tg220.htm For the Drug War results of 2010, see the continuously updated site at http:// en.wikipedia.org/wiki/Timeline_of_the_Mexican_Drug_War

13d.3 The World Great Depression II, 2008—Los Grandes Problemas Nacionales II [Urban and Rural Mexico in the World], 2006—Mexico is gravely impacted by the Wall Street-caused World Depression II, but the bright is that it has taken an event not seen since 1929 for it become clear to Calderón that a new vision is necessary. Figure 18 reveals the extent of the today's crisis as it interacts with historical crises to "demand" political change.

Thus, Calderón has called for limiting (and presumably later ending) Partidocracy in which Congressional positions are selected by the political parties. To succeed, accountability through direct election by the populace is necessary. With no possibility of reelection, voters have little chance to evaluate their "elected" Deputies and Senators at the outset because they are all chosen to run by the political parties, and they shift back and forth between the two chambers of Congress in between serving as Governor or head of an autonomous government agency.

The Calderón ACTIVE-STATE PLAN is comprehensive. For example, in 2009 he set out to begin ending subsidies to corrupt autonomous government agencies (such as Luz y Fuerza del Centro)[140] continue his effort to change the law, at least obliquely, so as to permit PEMEx to seek foreign help for the PEMEx (which will not be privatized but rather follower the Brazilian Model); begin to end Partidocracy by permitting re-election; rapidly adopt the right to oral trials, finally ending in Mexico the Napoleonic Code's "guilty until proven innocent"; "legalize" psychotropic drugs for personal and to be able to move freely with up to 3-5 days personal supply; restructure the mess at the Ministry of Health (which had not had the technology to identify the Swine Flu before it spread to all Mexico and the World in 2008; and (since 2006) sought to bring down the "Men with Guns" (the brutes seen in film director John Sayles movie of the same name) who have become "sub-human Beasts".

Too Calderón has to be sure that Mexico realize that the escape valve of workers going to the USA is now closed and many Mexicans returning on their own because of the U.S. unemployment crisis as well as deportation by Presidents Bush II and Obama—the latter deporting more than 2 million migrants by 2013.

To offset these problems, Calderon sought to build a Super-Port at Colonet, Baja California, so that world shippers could bypass inexpensively the complicated Ports of Los Angeles/Long Beach to reach rail lines into the USA.

Unfortunately, in the economic crisis of 2008 and 2009 and amid a Drug War, and other major problems, Calderón had to delay Colonet.

Calderón had to implicitly take on the problems that I list in Figure 18.

---

[140] http://www.internationalviewpoint.org/spip.php?article1759

FIGURE 18

MANY-PRONGED CRISIS, 2006-2010 LOS GRANDES PROBLEMAS NACIONALES II

STATUS OF THE FOLLOWING, which constitute OBSTACLES TO DEVELOPMENT

Oil reserves in collapse and Congress refuses to authorize entry under even under State control of foreign capital with expertise and rare deep-water rigs needed drill at least 20,000 feet below Gulf surface

Oil price collapse since 2008(but modest recovery end of 2010 offset by theft of oil and gas by PEMEx Sindicato, Narcotraficantes, and other criminals

> Foreign and domestic investment dramatic decline since 2008 with modest recovery since launch of Green Autos to be made in Mexico by U.S. and other foreign companies Remittances from workers in USA to families in Mexico from $25.1 billion in 2008 to $21.2 billion 2009, but perhaps (?) regained to $22.2 in 2010 http:// www.impre.com/laopinion/noticias/primera-pagina/2010/1/28/ bajan-las-remesas-a-mexico-170598-1.html and http://www. impre.com/laopinion/noticias/primera-pagina/2010/1/28/ bajan-las-remesas-a-mexico-170598-1.html#commentsBlock in tandem with

"Closure" of U.S. job market as an escape valve for Mexico's innovative and excess labor. Obama increases in 2009 raids on U.S. plants/ fields to increase deportations by at least 8% more than Bush II, raising the total to 388,000 (including families) for working/ being in USA without immigration documents.

Rise and fall of Mexican undocumented migrants in the United States (which stood at an estimated
2.2 million in 1980
12.0 million in 2006), fall to less than
11.0 million in 2009. http://www.migrationpolicy.org/pubs/IME-Jan2010.pdf
http://www.migrationinformation.org/datahub/countrydata. cfm?ID=482

IMSS (already underfunded for needed hospitals, medical/ staff, medicines/x-rays) collapsing under weight of non-members added by Seguro Popular (no worker contributions required)

Public Health System near collapse in 2009, owing to Swine Flu Crisis caused in Mexico and world by U.S. transnational Smithfield Farms

Public Health labs need to be upgraded to detect disease at outset, not weeks later affect samples sent to Canada and USA for first and second opinions

Dengue Fever sweeps 24 of Mexico's 32 states, over 45,000 cases in areas under 4,500 feet elev.

No vaccine against infected mosquitoes until perhaps 2014

> http://www.impre.com/laopinion/noticias/latinoamerica/2009/11/17/suben-alerta-por-dengue-en-mex-159350-1.html

Adult diabetes in Mexico is at "epedemic" levels: Mexican-American Migrants have been found to have 2x more propensity to fall ill with Diabetes 2 than "white non-hispanics (11.7% compared to 4.8%), owing to Indigenous genetics, heredity, intensive work style in the USA, and diet. See: http://www.impre.com/eldiariony/vida-estilo/salud/2010/12/12/una-vida-nueva-pero-con- diabet-227741-1.html#commentsBlock

Further, 73% of MexicanAmerican migrant woman are overweight and with Diabetes 2 compared to 61.6% of non Latinas in the USA. See http://www.impre.com/laopinion/noticias/primera-pagina/2011/1/2/el-suentilde;o-americano-les-r-231358-1.html#commentsBlock

Child health 35% of children under 12 are obese owing to excessive con- sumption of junk foods and high number of tortillas (many poor consume up to 17 tortillas daily—no meat, fish, milk, eggs, or even vegetables previously consumed in better times), addition to chips, breads and other carbohydrates, such as sugar-coated cereals and drinks, excessive use of the wrong cooking oils (e.g. beans refried in lard) lack of protein and exercise, etc., according to Mexico's Public Health Minister José Angel Cordoba, quoted in La Opinión, 1-13-10 www.impre.com/laopinion/noticias/latinoamerica/2010/1/13/engorda-en-mexico-mal-de- obesi-168210-1.html

Tourism to Mexico: arrival of foreigners subject to decline amid Drug Wars, kidnappings, and bouts of disease

Exports and Imports decline in the world "boom and bust" economy Transportation bottlenecks: hundreds of roads need to be made 4-lane and maintained; rail routes need to be double; tracked; heritage airlines are making international travel so high cost as to inhibit economic growth—and they have given up coastal flight to USA to U.S. airlines; monopoly domestic routes hurting tourism;

Construction industry decline

Agricultural production problems owning to
    worst drought (since 1938) in 2009-2010
    Mexico (like China, India, USA wastes and overuses ground water = declining resource http://www.sciencenews.org/view/generic/id/46322/title/Big_Gulp,_Asian_style
    decline in tourism cripples much agricul. production owing to collapse restaurant industry 2009-2010
    threats to cactus industry: theft of plants to sell in USA; nopa- lillo infection = some plants die
    still no federal agricultural extension
    lack of credit for ag producers as well as ejidos

Foreign Direct Investment decline

Credit availability to business and consumers ends; new credit cards and loans not generally available

"Reasonable" banking fees and interest has come to an end—"reasonable in Mexico can mean up to double that charged by U.S. banks

Notarial historical costs were supposed to be reformed but collapse of change makes legal transctions too costly for most persons (U.S. Notaries charge $5 to verify sigature on major documents; Mexican notaries charge % of transaction cost on theory they they are guaranteeing all the statements in the documents to be true

Implemenation of Title Insurance only beginning is few places and limited circumstancesComputerization of title recording developing too slowly

Consumer sales collapse since 2008

Business bankruptcy laws do not necessarily protect non-business property

Parti-docracy = Parties name 40% of the Deputies and 25% of the Senators, meaning that those "winners" do not campaign for votes of the population but only for power within their Party http://en.wikipedia.org/wiki/Senate_%28Mexico%29

No re-election means no accountability so Party holds control, not voters

Fatal political flaw = conflicting systems: Presidential, semipresidential, o parliamentary?—

Porfirio Muñoz Ledo notes; Mexico suffer from confusion of Spanish, French, U.S. laws, and Indigenous "usos y costumbres"

Government workers do not have civil service job protection: in most federal agencies and in most state and local "administrations" change in leadership results in wholesale change in job holders, thus disrupting knowledge about how the levels interact as well as the flow of work

Government ability to spend money—rigid expenditure rules ("normatividad") require dozens of signatures by bureaucrats at all level who fear being prosecuted if any kickbacks or corruption is later discovered—better not to sign

Government ability to spur business competition and regulate Monopolies is very low—a competitiveness commission exists but is powerless and frightened

Need to increase the terms of mayos from 3 to at least 4 years and change the complicated civil code that "freezes" actions by those mayors, who cannot afford the legal advice to keep them being charged with violation of rigid expenditure rules (normatividad)

Need for laws to regulating drug trade (except for legalization of relatively large amounts for "personal use" which already exits)

Need for effective, honest Police forces (which have always existed only in written plans) because low pay requires police to collect a living wage only by demanding bribes. Military pay is also to low to compete with Narcotraficantes

Judicial system continues to be hampered by corrupt use of amparo Judges subject to pressure ("convict and you and your family die") as in the 2010 Escobedo case where defendant confessed and led the police to the victim's remains—but he was released "for lack of evidence";"good sign" was the suspension of the judges and higher court reversal of the acquittal, "bad sign" was that it was too late to re-arrest the murderer, who had fled http://www.whatsonsanya. com/news-14041-mexican-victims-mum-marisela-escobedo-killed-too-while-demanding-justice. html

Serious need to reform prosecutorial, judicial, and prison systems: from Dec. 2006 to Dec. 2010, federal authorities made 540,000 pre-liminary investigations, prosecuted 400,000, and saw 82,500 persons imprisoned, a rate of only15% of the original total. See: http://www.impre.com/noticias/2010/12/17/son-36-mil-muer-tos-por-la-narc-228638-1.html#commentsBlock

Need to assess more cases in light of 2007 data that are not as positive: Of 100 Crimes, only 25 are reported and only 4.6 investigated,1.6 persons are prosecuted, and 1.1 persons sentenced to prison. See Guillermo Zepeda Lecuona, "Criminal Investigation and Subversion of Justice System Principles," on the internet as Judi- cial Reform in Mexico: Toward a New Criminal Justice System (2010), Table 3.

Need to verify data that indicate 400 persons have been extradited to the USA by Mexico between 2007 and 2010, 51 billion does of cocaine, heroine and marijana have been seized, at a total value of US$ 11.8 billion. See:http://www.impre.com/noticias/2010/12/17/son-36-mil-muer-tos-por-la-narc-228638-1.html#commentsBlock

Basic need to reform prisons to stop escapes: Man have fled from prison: in 2010, e.g., 351 persons escaped in the state of Tamaulipas (on the Texas border); and in 2009, 53 escaped in Zacatecas backed by narcotraficantes dressed as police, who entered the prison with a

17-car convoy and a helicopter; etc.... http://www.latimes.com/news/nationworld/world/la-fg-mexico-prison18-2009may18,0,4319828.story

Need to reform prisons, where prisoners rule—prisoners with cash can have a live-in wife or mistress and catered meals, use of cell phone, and easy access to drugs and weapons

Laws preventing kidnapping theoretically go into force in 2011 finally to define kidnapping in Mexico as starting from the first moment of forced detainment (rather than, say, 24 or 48 hours after the kidnapping, depending on how each state handles "Express Kidnappings"), but enforcement maybe difficult in the case of quick Express Kidnappings (often by police), and

"Bride kidnapping" (a term often applied loosely, to include any bride, usually a minor) 'abducted' against the will of her parents, because the young girl may be willing to marry the 'abductor' http://www.pittsreport.com/2010/12/mexico-2/http:// en.wikipedia.org/wiki/Bride_kidnapping

Lack of Innovation in industry, mining, and agriculture—most innovation now located in Brazil (Mexico's main competitor in Latin America)

Continuing foreign and domestic debt overhang totals 45% of GDP – including subtotal for FOBAPROA (1990) and IPAB (1998) which are up to 12% of GDP, according to Dr. Juan Moreno Pérez.

Compare Mexico's problems to the view by Andreas Kluth (the California correspondent for *The Economist*), who in 2010 saw California as the first failed state of the USA:

"If a state can no longer address or solve the problems it faces, then it has failed. California easily meets that criterion. Prisons: California has the worst recidivism rate in the country. Water: it's an infrastructure and a climate issue but it's also a governance issue. Education: California built the best public university system in the country, which it is currently dismantling because it is now a failed state. Budgets: a state is supposed to have a budget, to pass it on time, and California never does. That started well before the recession. Our opponents may argue that as soon as there's a recovery these problems will recede. It's not true. Warren Buffett says it's only when the tide goes out that you learn who's swimming naked. California has been undressing since the 1970s…since the infamous Proposition 13. This is something called direct democracy that the founders of the nation were very afraid of. Twenty-four states have [citizen] initiatives. Only one does not allow its legislature to amend initiatives that its voters have passed, no matter how insane. In only one state do the inmates run the asylum. http:// www.newsweek.com/id/232575 (1-26-10)

A major issue of the campaign was to bring an "end" to chaos created by criminals (narcotraficantes, kidnappers, and crooked police) and re-establish Government authority over the entire country. These are still major unresolved issues facing the country.

Although the PAN is anti-state in political terms, that is not the case in social terms. Calderón and the PAN sought unsuccessfully in 2007 to defeat the PRD legislation which has resulted in Federal District becoming the second federal entity in the country (after the state of Coahuila) to approve same-sex unions, and the first to allow conjugal visits for homosexual prisoners.

Most importantly, in 2007 under the PRD the D.F.'s Legislative Assembly expanded provisions on abortions, becoming the first federal entity to expand abortion in Mexico beyond cases of rape and economic reasons. The D.F. permits abortion, regardless of the reason, should the mother request it before week 12 of pregnancy.

Acting out of religious doctrine rather than legal policy, members of the Calderón government have set up a confrontation with the D.F. by refusing to permit federal hospitals in the D.F. to perform abortions, thus injecting the state into the private life of individuals.

Calderón faces the fact that PEMEx (the major source of income for the government) is exhausting Mexico's oil reserves and does not have the capability to drill in the deep Gulf of Mexico which has a huge oil reserve which it "shares" with the USA. Further, faces the same problem at the border with the USA, where Mexico shares an underground pool of oil with his neighbor to the north. (How the two countries share these pools of oil without one "draining" the other's share is not even being discussed.)

In the meantime, even though the PEMEx work force has been reduced by half during the Anti-State phase since 1983, it still has twice as many workers as needed, and 10% vacant, the pay of the phantom workers reverting to the PEMEx Union for its own activities. T/he Union itself holds "sweetheart contracts (guaranteed high-profit, low-yield results) with PEMEx.

The ability of Mexico's wealthy monopolists to defeat the federal government Competitive Commission is typified by the behavior of Carlos Slim, who has competed with Gates for the status of "richest person in the world." Unlike Gates (who has had his own problems of quashing the competition), Slim has donated virtually nothing to philanthropy—Gates donated US$ 30 billion. Slim's use of the amparo to prevent Mexico from forcing him to cut his incredibly high telephone rates is nothing short of criminal, say his critics. For the best analysis of Slim and his failure to invest ethically in Mexican business, see the public-service analysis by Denise Dresser: "Open Letter to Carlos Slim" (dated February 15, 2009): http://eacm.blogspot.com/2009/03/ open-letter-to-mexican-mogul-carlos.htm By preventing innovation and keeping costs high for poor service, Carlos Slim has almost single-handedly stunted Mexico's economic development. An anti-monopoly law had to be passed, and Calderon did pass the criminal justice reforms, fully implemented only in 2016.

Calderón has called for development of a new port at Colonet and a rail-road to link with the West-East railroad route from Los Angeles across the USA (thus relieving congestion at the ports of Long Beach and Los Angeles. But Mexico's complicated normative rules (see below) as well as the world financial crisis of late 2008 and 2009 that has dried up the flow of credit has plunged Mexico into more poverty.

For the PROFMEX-University of Baja California plan to develop the Baja Frontier as a Special Economic Zone to compete with China, see the Iniciativa UABC para la creación de la Frontera de Baja California-Global (FBC-GLOBAL 2030) como Primera Zona Económica Especial de México, by James Wilkie and Miguel Angel Rivera Rios.[141] Unfortunately, this project never came to fruition.

Calderón has been able to win a controversial tax reform from Congress, but it has alienated much of the private sector because businesses are taxed on gross receipts (not profits) and deductions are limited.

---

[141] See http://www.profmex.org/mexicoandtheworld/volume13/5latefall08/FBC- Global%2019a%20feb%2009.pdf

Mexico's real foreign debt of US$ 132 in 2008 (down from US$ 133 billion when he took office in 2006) is not a re al problem in making expenditure, but rather Calderón faces a tangle of Corporativist normative laws made more difficult by Fox's transparency laws that prevent expenditure of funds after he, the President has ordered that the expenditures be made. (Bureaucrats, who are authorized to make his expenditures, are always fearful of Congressional audits that will find them guilty of violating rules with "catch-22s." This serves to remind us of the near failure of John F. Kennedy when, purportedly, he ordered the Pentagon to "get the damned Jupiter missiles out of Turkey—they are threatening my deal with the Russians to get their missiles out of Cuba" (or words to that effect). Needless to say, it took six months to get the missiles out of Turkey, the Pentagon resisting to the bitter end.[142]

Calderón faces one positive situation in that the Mexican countryside has generally recognized that Mexico must spread the use of tractors. Where previous Presidents had failed to interest farmers to accept the plan to buy and distribute 10,000 tractors in Mexico, in 2007 the Confederación Nacional Campesino (National Peasant Federation) signed a contract to purchase 25,000 tractors from China.143[143] While the USA, Canada, Japan, and the European Union have 400 tractors for each 1,000 farmers, Mexico has only 12 tractors for each 1,000 farmers.[144] Calderon has also succeeded in fighting the narcos in 2007

---

[142] See www.abovetopsecret.com/forum/thread81277/pg1 and http://hnn.us/articles/7982. html

[143] See www.el-universal.com.mx/finanzas/58734.html

[144] See www.orizaba.info/orizaba/index/op/noticia/id/26047.html

Far behind Brazil and its use of sugar (which is far superior to corn) to provide bio-fuel at the pump, Mexico was only able to pass a law in 2008 that seeks to bring Mexico up-to-date:145 [145]Mexico's 2008 Law on Development of Bio-fuels establishes the basis for production, transportation, storage, distribution, and marketing of new fuels. It includes emphasis on protection of the environment and reduction of air pollution emissions. The Bio-fuels Law also establishes measures for protection of Mexico's self-supply of critical agricultural products, such as corn. The fight against the Narcos intensified with president Calderon. Felipe Calderón (2006-2012) was the first president to launch an all-out war on the narco kingpins, in conjunction with the American DEA. Where he should have protected the judges with a squad of soldiers. He had a lot of good ideas, created and established ProMéxico, and was aided by the U.S. DEA's in 2007. in the end, Calderon's fight against drug lords was a failure in fact. Genaro G. Luna (GGL), the General just launched his career under Calderón, by whom he was nominated Secretary of Public Security, a technical coordinator for Security operations. According to the Intercept, a news agency in the U.S., GGL has turned rogue sometimes in 2017, who had a proclivity to get bribes from El Chapo, as well as from the Cartel of Sinaloa, and from Beltran Levya. GGL had also paid President Pena Nieto 100.000 million dollars to stop chasing El Chapo Guzman. His secret name was LINSE. In Jalisco, and Guanajuato he filled up the penitenciaries with innocent people, and called this operation ironically, "Limpieza". There is a documentary on the "dark criminal", called "Sin Memoria," where his penal accusations were made public. In 2012 GGL was arrested finally in Texas, on four charges.

---

[145] See http://www.cailaw.org/iel_advisor/industry_news/lopez-velarde.almaraz_mexico_ biofuel.html

THE IMPORTANCE OF CIVIL SOCIETY IN MEXICO AND ROMANIA

The importance of activism, advocacy and agency work as main motors of a just and democratic society. Activism, civic engagement, voting are all happening online, on complex social media platforms like CISCO, Facebook, Twitter, LinkedIn.

It was Civic Engagement and activism, anti-totalitarian advocacy that really ended the Cold War. After the infamous explosion of the nuclear reactor in Chernobyl, and the cover up by the Soviets, investigative jour- nalism uncovered the misery of socialism, and harmful effects of propa- ganda going on behind the Iron Curtain.

The good old scholars of socialism, communism, have arrived to the conclusion at the beginning of this Millennium, that there was no civic polity in Eastern Europe whatsoever. But I am herein challenging this erroneous view.

Under communism the nations of Eastern Europe never had a civil society. A 'civil society' exists when individuals and groups are free to form organizations that function independently of the state, and that can mediate between citizens and the state.

Because the lack of civil society was part of the very essence of the allpervasive communist state, creating [civil] society and supporting organizations independent of the state--[such as] NGOs—have been seen by donors as the connective tissue of democratic political culture—First Eastern European to talk about civil society, empowerment of the citizens to counteract abusive governments was Michael Waltzer.

As of 1989 human rights advocates liked to imagine themselves as the "heroic underdogs" opposing the totalitarian autocratic government

- unofficial associations (including extended kin groups)

- informal interest groups (including traditional village families and mutual self-help groups),

- religious organizations (usually but not fully controlled by the party).

Romania has been led as a statist country under the dictatorship of Nicolae Ceausescu, and the Communist party (perfectly resembling the PRI, in Mexico). Over forty years of planned economy has been terminated by the shooting, execution style, of the dictator. And the bankruptcy of the country. Economically and morally.

In 2021, a privatized economy, Romania has attracted many Western inves-tors. After years of reeling from the statist leadership, after 1989, a a myriad of privatized holdings emerged, that belong either to the corrupt deep-state actors, or PSD (Social-Democrats) in the government. The PRD Party (much like the PRI in Mexico) is rotten to the core. Most of the state-held factories had been dismantled, or had been sold to foreign investors, Germany holding position number one i n investments into the Romanian infrastructure, as well as the European Union which offered tremendous help in improving the roads and historical monuments. But the infamous intelligence runs the country.

In Mexico, civil society has risen to counter the corrupt leadership of Pena Nieto and Lopez Obrador, and the insecurity due to the druglords'and narcos constant battle for territory.

Lydia Cacho is an investigative journalist who has exposed pedophiles in Mexico, and the state of Cancun corrupt political actors who put her in prison. Lydia actually had to leave the country for a few years. Ironically, the Amparo worked well in her case.

She is a successful civic actor, who succeeded in surviving the vengeful deep state in Mexico. According to recent developments, many activists and feminists think that civic society should be funded by the government, in order to point out where the prosecution is failing, not persecuted.

State and the Land in Mexico As of 2020, Mexico's 83% of the land had been in draught condition: it has been just too dry, and there is no water in the North West. Agricultural work is precarious in this conditions. NAFTA (or U.S. the Mexico_Canada Agreement,) signed in November 30th, 2018, is now called NAFTA 2.0. The U.S. is importing avocados, tomatoes, and other agricultural goods from Mexico. NAFTA is still in effect. But poor Mexicans allow to fester general corruption, lead by the president AMLO. The military and the police arecrooks. Also in the Yucatán Peninsula, the train rails he insists on building, disrupt the transfer of animals to the North, as cattle are just dying of thirst. Lopez Obrador says, "to hell with the animals, and the land." Three drug cartels are building an airport in Tulum, and it will be run by the army, at the air force base. AMLO has become a mad man. Instead of keeping in the pristine nature, he is destroying the environment, and placates feminism.

Cycles of statism, and anti-statism are a common thread that runs the narratives of two countries of immense beauty and stupendous climates.

Thank you for reading my book. If you liked this, read also: Civic Engagement, Civil Polity and Philanthropy in the USA, Romania and Mexico. **I like to think of this book as a precursor to Statism.**

For more titles, type in Olga Magdalena Lazin on Amazon.com Books, and follow. **For updates on this series, E-mail: olazin@ucla.edu**

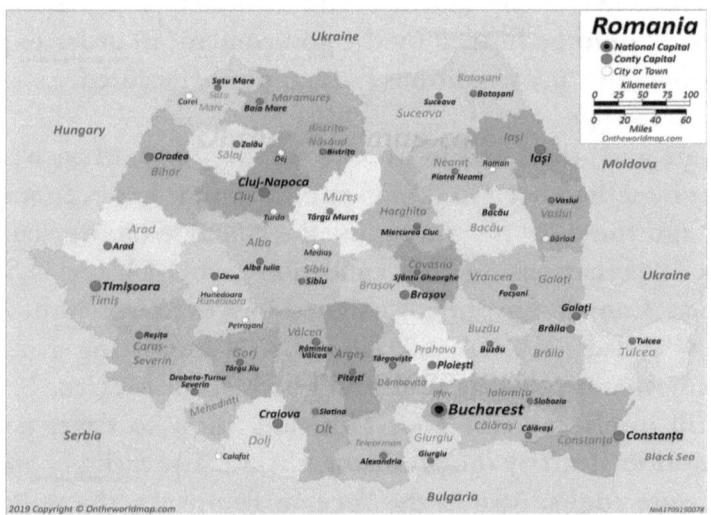

If you liked this book, read also:
"Civic Engagement, Civil Polity
and Philanthropy in the USA,
România and Mexico," 2017.
My Tweeter account: @AuOlgaLazin for Updates

ROMANIA HAS OVER 9 SECURITY AND INTELLIGENCE AGENCIES

At least nine security agencies are operating currently in Romanian. The number and functions of these units it is still unknown. The Romanian security service (SRI) -the main security infrastructure, is not subject to Parliamentary control, and actually there are not even Checks and Balances rules in place, other than SRI.

I identified unit number One, charged with **protection of the Presidency.** Unit Number two, which is the military unit, also called 0215- UM-0215.

Number 3 is the OPERATIVE SURVEILLANCE and INTELLIGENCE Directorate of the general Police Inspectorate (subordinated to the MAI, Ministry of Internal Affairs.

Unit number 4 is **the Foreign Intelligence Service,** and number 5 is the **Counter-Intelligence Directorate**, and the **Intelligence Directorate of the Army The Ministry of National Defence).** This intelligence structure is part of the of the MINISTRY of Justice. And number 6 is a **Special Telecommunications Service,** reporting only to the Military. The dreaded Securitate is still running the country and damaging the Romanian Psyche by working, and paying (read bribing), the magistrates, and lawyers. Statism and nationalism dominate Johan Klaus's rhetoric and policy ever since the pandemic has hit the country of Romania. This organizations could impel my country away from a democratic future. The BINOM case is an example, but this is the focus of our next series on "decentralized Globalization continuum, term that I coined in 2001, in my doctoral thesis with the same title.

Seealso:https://mexiconewsdaily.com/news/mexico-accuses-us-of-violating-mx-migrants-rights.`If you liked this book, part of a Series, see also the new waves of changes in DECENTRALIZED GLOBALIZATION: registered with the **Library of Congress, reg. # TX-8-662-05**

Chapter 27
Conclusion Without End: Pegasus

Statism and anti-statism as polarized states of government intervention, and interventioniusm will always oscillate between the two states, and will hardly ever be in equilibrium, especially in times of pandemic.

Mexico has spent $300 million Pesos in Israeli spyware by former security head Genarion G. Luna, and would have used the software for phone espionage against civil society. Pegasus is an Israeli spyware firm, widely used by Mexicans and Romanian governments.

The Mexican state has obtained the license to use surveillance software that is deadly against its own civic society actors. This book, and study, made across over 30 years of research, our study here illustrates why General Genaro Genario LUNA's dark assassin's story is the result of excessive use of surveillance and of the Pegasus project, and how his story ends in a jailhouse in New York, in the United States.

The head of security since 2000 has overstepped his boundaries, milked the state for decades, and has set up a state of terror against journalists, and civil society.

By using Pegasus against honest, crime fighting civilians, we can certify Mexico is a terrorist state.

The secret of Israeli NSO (software) is directly tied to head of CISEN (The Mexican Security agency) Genaro García Luna, who used technology against civilians, in order to extract money. Most corrupt official, GGL is in jail right now in New York.

Series Two Follows on Abuses. Read the next book.

TO BE CONTINUED

Source:
https://www.haaretz.com/israel-news/tech-news/.premium.HIGHLIGHT-the-secret-of-nso-s-success-in-mexico-1.9327961. #drolgalazin

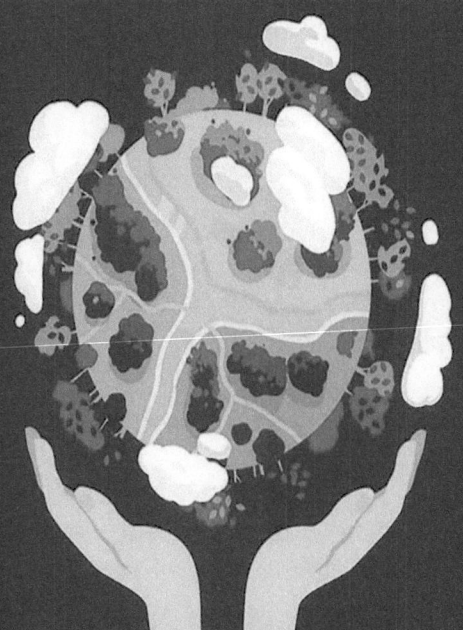

ORWELL'S "1984"

AND LIFE UNDER THE "BIG BROTHERS"

STALIN AND CEAUSESCU

by Olga M. Lazín

(PROFMEX Office for Eastern Europe)

1. The Orwellian Perspective on Power
- Language Abuse (Separation of Thought and Word)

II. Stalin's complex apparatus of mindcontrol

III. Personal experience under the Ceausescu'sdictatorship

IV. Conclusion

I

Orwell could detect the presence of power and the desire for it in minimal amounts and under camouflages that are concealed from most people.

In the last stage of his career he was preoccupied by the evils of totalitarian power.

"1984" pictures life thirty years hence under Ingsoc (English Socialism), a unit of Oceania, one of the three super-states in a permanent war for world hegemony. In the movie (1949) as well as in the book (1948), the piling up of detail upon detail of ashuddering, sickening; gripping spectacle of a human society is depicted stripped of the last shreds of community.

"1984" is the story of Winston Smith, a member of the outer Party, and his downfall which starts at the moment of first doubt crossed his mind. He works in Minitrue, the Ministry of Truth; he corrects past record when the present fails to bear out party predictions, deletes the names of men who have been "vaporized" and writes articles in 'Newspeak, which is the official language of Oceania.

Smith tasks are central to the state, for the party slogan is: 'Who controls the past controls the future, and who controls the present, controls the past.'

Ingsoc's Newspeak is designed to express the life of Oceania in the most fitting way to make all other modes of thought impossible. It contains words such as artsem (artificial insemination), Minitrue (Ministry of Truth) and Minipax (the ministry of peace) .

The Newspeak contains subtle concepts like crime-stop (halting one's expression just before it becomes dangerous) as well as the basic concept: doublethink (the ability to accept two contradictory expressions at the same time as true)

Members of the Inner Party invent 'doublethink' in order to manipulate the larger group, in the Outer Party, who are not always capable to understand such nuances and rarely master the full technique. The proles, eighty-five percent of the population, are incapable of any realthought.

All groups are capable of hate, which is constantly whipped up either by spectacle of mass hangings in the public square or by the image of Emmanuel Goldstein, the betrayer of the revolution... The fear created by the threats of Goldstein is overcome only by Big Brother, whose kindly black.-mustachioed face appears on the screens to efface the threatening Goldstein.

Winston's eyes are opened to the techniques of manipulation and the party's purpose by O'Brien, a member of the Inner Party who gives him a book which reveals the secret history of theparty.

In the end Winston is betrayed by O'Brian, who in reality is one of the heads of Thoughtpol. In a chapter unmatched in recent literature for the unrelenting description of inquisition and torture, Winston betrays Julia and himself. He not only confesses but finally comes to love the party and Big Brother.

The week Orwell's novel was published, the Sunday Times reported the call for a rival to newspeak: "model English," a new universal language 'with sentences having one word order and no idioms, with words having one meaning, one pronunciation, one spelling, one form and with letters having one sound and one shape.' This idea for this "model English" was invented by a University of Washington Sociologist, who saw the need for a law-abidinglanguage.

The Orwellian Newspeak lexicographers delete terms from the dictionary so that each word would have only one meaning, and that meaning would be compatible with the party line. Their goal is to make impossible any thought in conflict with the line.

The secret of the inner party is that it has mastered the usage of pure power.

The economy of the state is always a war economy. The head of the government is Big Brother, he of the ubiquitous face, whose all seeing eye follows one wherever there is light. The strong arm of power is the Thought Police; the greatest sin against the state, Crime think.

Once the secret of pure power is learned, Orwell suggests, the human being becomes completely malleable.

O'Brian is able easily to dispose of Winston's arguments against Big Brotherism by asserting that power is the reality of life. The arrests, the tortures, the executions, he says, will never cease. The heresies of Goldstein will live for ever, because they are necessary to the Party. The Party is immortal, and it lives on the endless intoxication of power.

In the end, Winston willingly inclines to obey O'Brien, and in the point of no return (becomes malleable). The corrosion of the will through which human freedom is worn away is well illustrated through the telescreen (the ubiquitous eye), which receives and transmits simultaneously, is fitted into every room of every member of the Party. The telescreen can be dimmed but not turned off, so that there is no way of telling when the Thought Police have plugged in on any individual wire.

Is this our world-to be? Is this Socialism? Or is the creation of a central intelligence agency in any country of the world, with the power to plant agents in every voluntary association in the country (including trade/labor unions) or in people's houses (by recruitment of informers)? The imaginary country Oceania is a metaphor for the 'enemy of the People' which justifies any dictatorial/arbitrary action of the government. It is the 'enemy' that didn't even exist but was invented to justify decision making control of minds and actions of the party.

One of Orwell's best strokes is his analysis of 'double-think', drilled into the party members, which consists of the willingness to assert that black is white when the Party demands it, and even to believe that black is white, while at the same time knowing very well that nothing of the sort can be true. Thought marked by the acceptance of gross contradictions and falsehood, especially when used as a technique of self-indoctrination: "Doublethink ... is a vast system of mental cheating'," says Orwell.

Although it might seem improbable that "1984" could exist in the 1980s, let me draw upon my own experience to illustrate that the impossible wording and 'Doublethinking' of Nineteen Eighty-Four was (and often still is) present in every sector of the ex Soviet and Romanian society. Nor is it a technique available exclusively to Soviet or Romanian citizens only.

II. Stalin and The Totalitarianlinguistics

Let me start with Stalinist Russia where real Newspeak. was generated and evolving and has been successfully replicated in the Eastern European countries, those 'behind the Iron Curtain' drawn by Stalin after W.W.II.

Stalin (originally Joseph V. Dzhugashvili, the successor of Lenin) succeeded in creating during his rule from 1922 to 1953 a myth making system that rivals that of Big Brother's power. Stalin's system of mind control was so effective that millions of Russians were staged and paraded in front of him eulogizing him as being godlike - and all the nation trembled at his feet.

Since the time of Nero, the Roman king who liked spectacles which involve masses of people acting as one, social uniformity, all dictators were fond of parades. Stalin's propaganda chief Andrei Jidanov knew and brought to perfection the organization of the parades.

Stalin, or the paterfamilias, was praised through the press, radio, cinema, music and the performing arts. Stalin was experimenting in mind control by designing an Orwellian nation of idol worshipers, who were cut off from outside influence, told and told again that Stalin was good, the source and provider of all things and the one who loves them.

Maxim. Gorki, the Head of the union of the writers, was called upon to perfect Stalin's language machine. In the documentary film "Monster: Portrait of Stalin in Flesh and Blood" Maxim Gorki is shown asking the writers not to write poorly, because writing "poorly is not to praise Stalin and his achievements."

One of Stalin's theatrical "achievements" was at the White Sea Baltic Canal, where one of his notorious labor camps was located and where "performers" (prisoners on forced labor) were carefully orchestrated in staging penitent work as happy labor to influence the thinking of visiting writers. Thus Gorki could exclaim: "Labor sets the prisoner free." One can recognize here the Orwellianlanguage:

"FREEDOM IS SIA VERY"

"IGNORANCE IS STRENGTH"

"WAR IS PEACE"

These were three slogans of the party in "1984".

After viewing and believing this pathetic charade (at the White Sea Baltic Canal), the visiting writers glorified the righteousness and decency of the Soviet justice system. Perhaps they were influenced by the fear as they had witnessed the fate that would otherwise be them. Poets and writers who resisted, opposed or doubted Stalin's "perfection" were sent to rot in the gulags (labor camps in Ljubianka and Siberia). Therefore every word written or uttered in public was pure orthodoxy.

Stalin's mind control apparatus also turned westward. Famous writers like G. B. Show, H. D. Wells, A. Gide, R. Roland arrived and received a heroes welcome to Russia. They were shown the grandiose facade of communism and not its shabby underside.

Stalin was a masterful manipulator of his image as he set out to perform all the spectacles and by extension we might think that he was the incarnation of Big Brother even to the mustaches.

III. My personal experience or the Romanian version of "1984"

Well before the composition of Nineteen fourty-eight, however, totalitarian countries had produced what were, in effect, workable versions of Newspeak. The totalitarian linguistics can often do (up to a point) by non-violent means what the instruments of the torture chamber do by violent ones. Thus, while wisdom is often hidden in the meaning of the words, so is error.

Just over Russia's border, In Romania, under the Ceausescu dictatorship (1965-1989), the language of the state became what we secretly called a "wooden language," a meaningless speech deliberately ambiguous and evasive so as to confuse themasses.

Romania was for years the private estate of the Ceausescu family (30 members in the government), much as Trujillo's former Dominican Republic and the Somoza's old Nicaragua were ruled by nepotism.

In the Romanian variation of state terror, the nation could progress only under socialism; the party represents not the international working class but the nation. Party membership requires total devotion and loyalty to the leadership. The Communist Party hierarchy standing over the state and society, became a mass organization subordinate to the state. Party and state functions became much more extensively merged than in the Soviet Union. Romanians had to swear loyalty to both state andparty.

The strongest fusion was at the top. Ceausescu was at once General Secretary of the Party, President of state, President of the State Council and Chairman of the National Defense Council on Socioeconomic Development. His personality cult was the strongest in the communist world exceeded only by that of Kim II Song in North Korea.

To understand what Ceausescu meant for the Romanians, however, I have to concede his merit at the early stages of leadership. Ceausescu won popular support when he refused to take Romania into the Soviet run COMECON (Council for Economic Assistance), claiming that becoming subservant to COMECON was inadmissible for a Communist state, offensive to the pride as well as injurious to the Romanian economy. Ceausescu also asserted a limited independence in defense and foreign policy. He declined to let Romania participate in joint military maneuvers on Romanian soil and restricted military integration into Soviet military activity.

The critical rise to power for Ceausescu came in 1968, when he refused to join in the Soviet invasion of Czechoslovakia Ceausescu, who had succeeded the deceased Gheorghiu-Dej in 1965, proclaimed that Romania would forcibly resist invasion: the Communist Party thereby became truly popular and the cult of the personality of Ceausescu was born.

Nevertheless nationalism and authoritarianism came together in forced industrialization in the Stalinist manner; Ceausescu's brand of socialism consisted in the devotion of the maximum percentage of the national product to investment. There had been no retreat from central planning in industry or agriculture.

A strong myth-building machine was set in function by the designers of public celebrations. Parades became ritualistic eulogies of the Communist Party and songs and poems were all dedicated to "the brave, beloved 'conducator' Nicolae". As center of a small elite of loyalists who run the country, his image was everywhere, and the banners proclaimed not only, or not primarily the Communist

Party but the name of Ceausescu. The servile writers and poets who supported Nicolae, were then sent on trips abroad and were guaranteed momentary immunity.

The infamous Romanian 'Securitate' performed as the "Thoughtpol': this 'eminence- grise' was ever-present and patrolled almost every street. Informers told the 'Securitate' who was listening to the radio 'Free Europe' and what professors were teaching. in school. The irony of the term like 'Securitate' or Security is intuitively relevant to our lives. By the end of the regime computer-kept records could be revised with an ease that Winston Smith would not have been able to imagine. Members of the Security were invested with the cutting edge of technology' and were arbitrarily arresting anyone who was suspicious or had been "reported".

Writers, potential leaders or defectors were brutally tortured, imprisoned, or mysteriously "vaporized". Much of the technology of the fictional "1984" was in all Nicolae Ceausescu's years in power.

As in "1984" Ceausescu ordered that TV monitors should be placed on each comer of major streets in central Bucharest so that the military could intervene in an effective and timely way to prevent any popular uprising. Groups of more than 4 people were prohibited by law, unless under government control. Complete isolation from exterior influence was imposed as a measure of 'protection' of the Romanian nation from the imperialistic powers.

TV was limited for 25 years to a sole national channel, reported with spurious accuracy false statistics, systematically distorting the people's ability to understand the miscontrolled economy. Nicolae and his wife Elena were shown as a happy presidential couple daily visiting towns, villages, and fields with the peasants. They were shown reviewing the 'socialist achievements' in the factories, holding kids in their arms and expounding mealy-mouthed slogans about government benevolence and personal sacrifice made by the officials, the pain they underwent for the Romanian people. Nicolae and Elena Ceausescu were so megalomaniac that painters, carpet wavers and sculpturers were ordered to imprint the Ceausescu's images everywhere. Elena C's wardrobe contained as many dresses as that of Evita Peron. The couple had a palace in every city /resort of the country.

In their daily speeches the Ceausescu's were more Romanian than all Romanians, all science was 'Romanian', gymnastics and soccer were best Romanian, as were bread, butter and salt, everything good was Romanian. Ceausescu Nicolae became the supreme leader - who told his people what to eat (food was rationed), what to wear (depending on the weather,) and how many children a family should have (abortion being punished with imprisonment).

The Palace of the People, built with enormous sacrifices by Ceausescu's order and in his 'honor' is still the second enormous building in Europe after Versailles.

After 1975 all foreign journals and magazines were banned from entering the country. Among the weekly laws promulgated by Ceausescu, one prohibited answering foreigners' questions. Foreign visiting relatives had to stay only in controlled hotels. This law was an absolute aberration for philology students or professors as no communication was possible in other languages than Romanian.

The academic milieu and curricula was infested with Marxist ideology. The following terminology dominated all life: "the new man" , "revolutionary", "socialist competition", "multilaterally developed society". People addressed each other as 'comrades'. The continuing influence of socialism on the language of intellectuals and scholars was evident also in the textbooks, in every discipline. To Marx especially we owed the substitution of the term "society" for the "state." This circumlocution suggested that the actions of individuals can be regulated by some gentler and kinder method of direction than coerdon. As a result, the Communist system rooted out civilsociety.

Having antagonized some professors which were using this "wooden language" of communism, I came under the scrutiny of the "Securitate" and even dared to laugh in the face of a Security officer who was assigned to read the mound of absurd decrees newly promulgated by the government. My tenure at the University was henceforth compromised, and I resolved to flee Romania, an illegal act initself.

Caught at the border with ex Yugoslavia, I was incarcerated for one year (1986-1987). Ironically there was no social stigma to being jailed because the whole country was considered "The Jail."

After Ceausescu was toppled in a coup by a clan of his acolytes during a parallel popular revolution in 1989, I was finally allowed to complete my degree in philology at the University of Cluj-Napoca.

IV. Conclusion

The infernolike atmosphere of the "1984" story is cunningly created and it calls to my mind images of urban industrialized cities tailored after Ceausescu's mind in the 1980s.

Both my personal experience and the ending of Orwell's novel are meant to be a warning against the extremes to which totalitarian spirit can carry us, so that we will understand dangers involved wherever power moves under the guise of order andrationality.

I personally consider that it is an extraordinary time to analyze in this film based on the novel- about ambition, greed and power in an apparently endless battle for political control going on in the entireworld.

If we do not think, there could be many who will be more than willing to do it for us. Constant vigilance is the cost of our freedom.

The Hierarchy of the Orwellian Society in "1984"

O'Brian ——— Thought Police ——— Crime Think

Big Brother

Double Think   Inner Party   Doublespeak

W.Smith   OuterParty   Newspeak Proles

Hate   hate   hate

ENEMY

OCEANIA

CONCLUSION
WITHOUT END

Surprise? The PRI is the 2010 favorite to win back the Presidency in 2012. The PRD has splintered, badly damaged by the antics of AMLO, who is seen as hopelessly out of touch with reality, even in the Party that he led from 1996 to 2009—13 years attempting to become a new Jefe Máximo smashed his personal reputation.

Although the PRI lost the Presidency to the PAN in 2000, the PRI's system of "Corporativism" remains largely in place at the federal level as well as at the State and Town/City/County levels of government to prevent much of the change that Anti-Statists and Active Statists have sought to implement. By the time of the PRI's 75th anniversary in March 2004, the PRI could claim that it held 37% votes cast nationally—a percentage that understated its power and the power of the Corporativist system that it left in place.

In early 2009 the PRI held 52% of the Mexico's 32 governorships, 38% of the 31 state legislatures (31 excludes the D.F), and 37% of the country's 2,457 mayorships. Thus, the PRI has more governorships and more control of legislatures and mayorships than any other political party. See the PRI website in English www.pri.org.mx/PriistasTrabajando/PRIen- Mexico/english.aspx

Given the unpopularity of the PAN owing to the long Drug War and taxation changes in the face of the resurging PRI, in 2010 the PAN moved toward an alliance with the new PRD, which had seen AMLO for the leftist

Partido de Trabajo (PT). AMLO hoped to split the PRD and make the PT into the new power on the left, but all this did was drive the PRD and PAN into each other's arms as they looked for ways to beat the PRI in coalitions such as developed in Sinaloa (where the PRI lost the governorship for the first time in 81 years. The same alliance was also successful in Oaxaca, which also finally saw the PRI loose the governorship after 81 years.

Most observers think that the PAN has no viable candidate for Mexico's Presidency in 2012, but perhaps Diego Fernández de Cevallos ("El Jefe") has "saved the day", some argue. He was "kidnapped" in May and released in December 2010, supposedly having "negotiated the ransom down from US$ 100 million to $ 30 million. But the "victim", who will be 71 in March 2011, appeared to be in such good shape after more than seven months in captivity that speculation began: He had arranged a "self-kidnapping" to help create sympathy for the PAN, for which he ran as presidential candidate in 1994. El "Jefe Diego" has said nothing about his captors, but a branch of the EzLN claimed in a message to Mexico that he had been held at the orders of former Sub-Comandante Marcos, who had seemingly disappeared from the scene. Claiming in their message that they are the "Ex-Mysterious Kidnappers", they took him hostage as the arch-leader of Neo-Liberalism and enemy of the Indigenous People.

At this writing, conspiracy theory is rising. What does all this mean, which is the tone for example of new articles, for example, by EFE (the Spanish News Agency based in Madrid), which referred to the "supposed message from the 'EzLN' and the "link" to Marcos.[1]

---

[1] Secuestro de Fernández 'por EzLN,'" *La Opinión*, January 2, 2011.

Felipe Calderón, inaugurated December 1, 2006, believes that Corporativism must be ended along with the costly and inefficient remainders of Statism (such as the PEMEx and electricity monopolies), but he cannot say so directly owing to PEMEx being seen by many as the symbol of Mexican economic independence in the world.

Yet Calderón did take on Sindicato Mexicano de Electricistas main operations in the center of the country, in October 2009 abolishing their power over the company and installing real accounting. (Rogue agents of the SME are still blowing up power transformers to claim that no other experts can maintain them like the experts of the SME.)

Unfortunately for Calderón, his administration has coincided with World Depression II, and many voters do no understand the complicated international relationships that have brought major economic problems to all countries of the world

Others argue that "Statism" is not the issue but rather the development of an "Active State" that can take care of the population unprotected by the "free market," which needs serious regulation to stop the greed of CEOs willing to destroy entire economies for their yearly bonus that is based on failure if not success.

The Narcotraficantes continue to fin d themselves splintered into internecine warfare among competing cartels, trying to stay alive and if in jail not extradited to the USA. In the meantime they constitute a threat to Mexico's self-confidence and safety of the general public. With law- lessness seemingly on the rise, kidnappers (be they Narcotraficantes, police, and/or independent criminals) have emerged to hamper the role of domestic and foreign tourism in Mexico, in 2009.

Statism, It's Recurring Cycles In Mexico And Romania

Mexico is not a "failed State," as the Pentagon suggested in 2009, but one in which Narcotraficantes seek a state of anarchy in relation to police and military ability to stop their activities. See Map 4 for the sway of six areas where at least seven cartels struggle with each other and with the Mexican government. We now know, general GGL worked withBut the very fact that Calderón has been able develop a vision, which I articulate here as "Los Grandes Problemas Nacionales II, augers well for Mexico attempting to resolve problems, including dozens of Obstacles to Development (age-old half-solved, half-understood, and accumulating faster than any can be "solved" is based on the realization, I hope, that we all recognize that there are no final solutions, but only adaptations to history as it advances into the present—always subject to re interpretation in the light of new events and findings.

Morever, about Statist abuses in Mexico by elites: AMLO (2018-2024) and his security agency, with his Movimiento de Regeneración Nacional (MORENA) Political Party attempts to "re-nationalize" many of the big industries such as OIL, Ports, Airports, Electricity, Railways, etc., as he seeks to end independent investigations by his "centralization of government", wherein he seeks to absorb the governments own autonomous agencies to shift their investigations to be under his own personal power. AMLO saved Gen. Salvador Cienfuegos from U.S. Federal Court where he was indicted in 2020 for having worked in concert with Mexican and U.S. drug dealers, AMLO claiming that he would be tried by Mexico. Back in Mexico, the General was freed upon arrival in 2021, even before AMLO "read" any of thousands of pages of CIA and FBI documents that had arrived with Cienfuegos. Then the "trial" or investigation never took place because AMLO claimed that the USA had concocted made-up Charges. Thus, AMLO quickly blocked all Mexican Agents from meetings with U.S. agents unless they send to the Mexican Minister of Foreign Relations recordings and memos about what was discussed, thus effectively blocking contact. AMLO ended the "rights" of the FBI, CIA, etc.

to carry guns for self-defense in Mexico. And AMLO broke the U.S.-Mexico Treaty by throwing some secret U.S. documents into the air to reveal ("inadvertently"?) to Mexican criminals some top secret information that could only help them learn how, where, and with whom U.S. agents operate. His case could have affected AMLO's safety, hence his need for (a) getting Cienfuegos out of the USA, and (b) making an angry "attack" on FBI and CIA operations in Mexico for having made "no case against the General." We are focusing on what is the next Great Crisis for Mexico under AMLO. Security for certain.

You can find the author OLGA LAZIN on:

Twitter: @olgamlazin
stagram: #drolgalazin
On Facebook: Dr. Olga Lazin
My Books: http://www.olgalazin.com/books.html
Civic Engagement
Civil Society

And Philanthropy in The USA
Romanian & Mexico

OLGA MAGDALENA LAZIN

UCLA POST-DOCTORAL FELLOW, 2001-2004

Office Address

PROFMEX
3180 Sawtelle Blvd, Apt 103
Los Angeles, CA 90066

Tel. (310) 208 7914
Fax (310) 208 4918
Cell: (310) 488 0061
E-mail: olazin@ucla.edu

Dual Citizenship: USA and Romania   Born: November 4, 1963

Education

2001-- Post-doctoral Fellow in Latin American Studies, UCLA
2001   Ph.D. in History, UCLA
1996   M.A. in History, UCLA
       B.A. in Philology, Bolyai University, Cluj, Romania

Professional Service: PROFMEX (Worldwide Consortium on Mexico)

1997 -- Editor, Web Journal, *Mexico and the World*
http://www.profmex.com

1994-- Director, NAFTA-European Integration
1989-- Director For Latin American Studies)

Author, Books:

*Decentralized Globalization:
Free Markets, U.S. Foundations, and the Rise of Civil* and *Civic
Society from Rockefeller's Latin America to Soros' Eastern Europe*

In press, to appear in Spring, 2004, published by the University of Guadalajara, UCLA Program on Mexico, and Juan Pablos Editores

Book in Progress:

*Mexico's First and Second Green Revolutions
Super Wheat and Double Protein Corn for the World*

Articles:

2003 "La carrera mundial hacia los bloques de libre comercio", in *Publicationes de UNAM* 24, pp. 8-20.

2002 "Expansion del Papel del Instituto Nacional de Migración de México (INAMI) y Establecimiento de Un 'Think Tank" Dedicado a Mejorar la Calidad de Vida en La Gran Los Angeles-Tijuana," (México, D.F.: INAMI, 2002), Chapter 5.

2001 "History and Components of Globalization," *Statistical Abstract of Latin America* 37 (Los Angeles: UCLA Latin American Center Publications), pp. xxiv-xxvii.

2000b "Romanian Globalization Theory and Its Impact In Latin America - The Neopopulist Discourse," *UCLA Historical Journal* 19, pp. 12-34.

2000a Review of Joseph Love's *Crafting the Third World: Theorizing Under-development in Brazil* (Stanford University Press, 1996), in Web Journal *Mexico and the World* 5:2 www.isop.ucla.edu/profmex/volume5/2spring00/00Lazin1.htm

1999b "Mexico and Romania Compared," in *Mexico and the World*, edited by James W. Wilkie (México, D.F.: PROFMEX-ANUIES), pp. 206-233. Also in Web Journal *Mexico and the World* 6:1www.isop.ucla.edu/profmex/volume6/1winter01/01lazin1.htm

1999a "Globalización Fast-Track y el Surgimiento de Áreas de Libre Comercio (ALC) y Corporaciones Transglobales (CTG) Virtuales", in *México Frente a la Modernización de China*, ed. Oscar M. González Cuevas (México, D.F.: Universidad Autónoma Metropolitana-Unidad Azcapotzalco), pp. 307-359.(Co-authored with James W. Wilkie)

1996 "Bloques Emergentes de Comercio Internacional: Comparación Entre el Área de Libre Comercio de América del
Norte y la Unión Europea," *Carta Económica Regional*, Universidad de Guadalajara, No. 48, May-June, pp. 29-36.

1995b "NAFTA and The European Union Compared," *Statistical Abstract of Latin America*, Vol. 31 Part 2, pp. 1205-1230; Reprinted in Web Journal *Mexico & the World* 2.2 (1997) http://www.isop.ucla.edu/profmex/webjournal.htm

1995a "México Como Punta de Lanza para el Libre Comercio en las Américas," in *Ajustes y Desajustes Regionales*, eds. Jesús Arroyo Alejandre y David E. Lorey (Guadalajara y Los

Angeles: University of Guadalajara y UCLA Program on Mexico), pp. 47-112.
(Co-author James W. Wilkie)

1994 "Mexico as a Linchpin for Free Trade in the Americas," in *Statistical Abstract of Latin America*, Vol. 31:2, pp. 1173-1203. (Co-author James W. Wilkie); also in Web Journal *Mexico & the World*, Vol. 31, Part 2 (Fall 1996) pp. 1173 to 1221.

1985 "Originality and Stereotypes," *Nord*, Baia Mare, Romania, Jan, p. 3.

1989 "Confessions," *Nord*, Philology Department, Baia Mare University, Romania, January 1, p. 5.

Teaching Experience: Lecturer

2003 Cerritos College,
History of the United States and Its Constitution,
History 101 (Two Sections), Fall Semester

2003 UCLA,
The Mexican Films of Luis Buñuel,
History XLC 170A, Summer Session,
Co-taught with James Wilkie

2003 UCLA,
Issues in Latin American History: Globalization Since 1492,
Extension, History XL 170C, Summer Quarter

2003 UCLA,
History of Mexican Film,
Extension, History 170C, Spring Quarter

> My Invited Guest: Alejandro Pelayo, Cultural Attaché of Mexico

2002 California State University, Dominguez Hills,
> The Individual, Family and Community in Historical Perspective, History 301.1, Fall Semester, Spring Semester, Summer Session

2002 California State University, Dominguez Hills
> History of the World, History 121, Summer Session

2002 Santa Monica College.
> The Mexican Revolution Since 1910, History 19, Spring Semester

2002 California State University, Dominguez Hills, Women and Globalization," Women's Studies Course, 401I, Spring Semester.

2002 California State University, Long Beach,
> World History Since 1500, History 212, Spring Semester

2001 Santa Monica College,
> Modern Mexico & the Mexican Revolution, History 5, Fall Semester

2001 California State University, Dominguez Hills,
> Women in World History, History 380, Fall Semester Fall Semester

2000 Santa Monica College,
> History of Mexico,
> History of Latin America,
> Summer Quarter

1999 Cerritos College,
　　　　History of the Americas,
　　　　History 8.1, Winter Quarter

1999 UCLA
　　　　Many Images of Mexico,
　　　　History 171, UCLA Spring Quarter,

UCLA Course Teaching Assistant: Department of History

2004　　　　　　Cultural History of Mexico (170C)

1997-9998　　　Historical Statistics of Latin America (Graduate: 268A-B)

1994　　　　　　Leaders in World Development (169)

1993 - 1994　　Latin American Film and Society (170A)

1999　　　　　　Classic Travel Accounts of Latin America (History 170C)

1999　　　　　　Colonial Mexico (8A)

Course Readers Edited

2003　Mexico's Film History

2002　Women in International Advocacy Movements: Globalizing Women in History, California State University, Dominguez Hills

1999　*Frontiers in Elitelore,* UCLA History 169

1995　*Issues in Elitelore and Folklore,* UCLA History 169

Research Awards from UCLA International Studies Overseas Programs

1999-2001 UCLA, ISOP Travel Grant to Conduct Research on "Reconstructing the Legal Framework For Civil Society in Romania: The Mexican Model."

1997-1998 UCLA Travel Grant to Conduct Research on "Women and Civil Society in Europe

1996 Latin American Center Fieldwork Award

Professional Leadership

2000 PROFMEX-UCLA Conference Organizing Committee,
"Mexico and Public Policy," Morelia, State of Michoacán,
September 19-25.

1998 Conference Organizer: "The Latina Woman in Film,"
UCLA, May 1998.

1997 PROFMEX Conference Organizing Committee, "Mexico and the World," Morelia, State of Michoacán,
December 8-15
www.profmex.com //mexworld/issue6/art1

1993-- Organizer, NPPOs GLOBAL-Program for Legally Facilitating the Flow
of U.S. - Based Tax Exempt Funds to Not-For-Private-Profit
Organizations Worldwide. Conferences held in:

               Belgium, Hungary, Romania, 1998
               Hungary, Romania, Switzerland, 1994
               France, Russia, Spain, 1993

1993   Chief of Mission, Establishment of PROFMEX Office at the Institute of Latin American Studies, Russian Academy of Science, Moscow June 15-26.

1992   Director NAFTA - European Integration Studies, based in France and Mexico, February 20-December 15.

1991   PROFMEX Organizer, "Mission to Analyze De-statification in Eastern Europe," September 15 – October 12.

Memberships

American Historical Association 1998

Conference on Latin American History (CLAH), 1998 --

PROFMEX–Consortium for Research on Mexico

Board of Directors, 1997—

California Faculty Association, Latino Caucus, 2001

UCLA Alumni Association, Life Member, 2001--

Holmby Park Advisory Board, Beverly Hills, 2001--

Northern California Translators Association (NCTA), 2000--

Feminist Majority Foundation (Founder, Feminist Alliance, UCLA Chapter), 2000

Conferences, Seminars Presentations and Invitations:

2003   American Historical Association:
Paper "The Health Education and Communications Index in Latin
American Countries," January 12-17, Chicago

2002c   UCLA-UNAM Conference on Human Rights:
Paper: "Mexican Migrants in the USA and Human Rights Issues in Latin America," November 12, Dashew Center

2002c   IEEE (Communications, Computers and Electronic Engineering) Conference IEEE, Acapulco, paper on "The Social Impact of E-Networking in a Globalized World," Acapulco, October 1-6,

2002b   Southwest Feminist Leadership Institute,
Chair, "International Family Planning and the Global Gag Rule,"
Los Angeles, March 1

2001b   International Education Association
Conference on Latin American Literature and Education, Paper: "The Challenge of Globalization, Civil Society in Latin America and Canada." Mexico City, June 17-24

2001a   Conference on "Urban Poverty Worldwide," Toluca, State of Mexico, November 6-9, Paper: "Marginalization of Women in the Labor Force."

2000b   Conference Organizer Technological Knowledge and Women's
Role in the Global Advocacy Networking," UCLA, June 4

2000a	PROFMEX-UCLA Conference on Mexico and Public Policy, Paper: "The Mexico NGO Sector and the Role of Women." Morelia, Michoacán, Mexico, Sept. 14– 23. TV Interview: Noticiero Canal 13, Televisa National Program Mexico/USA coverage
1999	UCLA Colloquium in European History and Culture, Paper: "Globalization of Civil Society: "The Open Society Fund in East-Central Europe– International Philanthropy" October 16
1999	PROFMEX-Guanajuato Conference on Innovative Ideas for Mexico's Development, Paper "The Role of Transnational NGOs in Developing Civil Society in Mexico," Guanajuato City, April 14-19.
1999	U.S. Small Business Association Seminar at UCLA: Chair, "Globalization and Romania's Transylvanian Region," July 7.
1999	American-Romanian Academy Paper: "International Advocacy Networks From Local to Global", University of Oradea, Romania, March 15-20.
1997	Romanian Academy Conference, Paper: "Civic Society and the Transfer of the Mexican-U.S. Model to Romania," Cluj Napoca, Romania, June 15,
1997	Romanian Civic Academy Conference on Rebuilding Civil Society, Paper: "The Deliberate Distraction ofRomania's Civil Society after 1947 by the Ceausescu Dictatorship," Sighet, Maramures, Romania, June 22

1996	UCLA Colloquium on Romania, Paper: "The Emerging Romanian Informational Infrastructure," June 17
1996	UCLA Colloquium in European History and Culture, Paper: "Civil Society and the Mexican Adaptation of the U.S. Philanthropic Model," October 16,
1995	The American-Romanian Academy of Science Annual Meeting, Moderator: "Session on Culture" Paper: "Orwell's '1984' and Life Under 'Big Brothers' Stalin & Ceausescu," University of Reno, January 12-17
1994	PROFMEX Policy Seminar for Managing the Greater El Paso- Ciudad Juárez Metropolitan Area, Paper: "Simplifying U.S.-Mexican Visas," El Paso, March 14-15.
1994	Mexico's Federal Electoral Institute, Invitee as International Observer of the Mexican Presidential Election, Mexico City, August 19-22.
1994	PROFMEX Conference on Experiences of De-statification Paper: "NAFTA and EU Compared," Mexico City, August 23, 1994
1995	Romanian Internet Learning Workshop. Paper: "Ironies and Complexities of Redefining Civil Society In East-Central Europe." Miercurea Ciuc, Romania, April 29, http://oc1.itim-cj.ro/rilw/Papers/Olga.html

1993 Mexico City University (UAM-A),
Lecture: "Accelerating the Education of Young Women in Mexico:
A Development Imperative," September 18,

Languages Spoken and Written

English - speak, read, write
Romanian - speak, read, write
French - speak, read, write
Spanish - speak, read, write
German - speak
Latin - read, write
Hungarian - speak, read, write
Italian - speak, read, write

Travel and Research

Europe   Americas
Austria: Sept 1991
Canada: Oct 1992, Nov 1995
Belgium: Sept 1995
Mexico: Yearly, 1992--
Bulgaria: Sept 1992
England: Jan and May 2001
France: 1991-1992
USA: October 1992--
Hungary: 1991, 1992, 1995, 2002
Guatemala, January 1999
Romania: Yearly, 1992--
Costa Rica, March 1999
Russia: June 1993
Spain: March 1992
Switzerland: June-July 1994
Turkey: July 2000

References

James W. Wilkie, UCLA Professor of Latin American History
Chair, UCLA Program on Mexico, 6299 Bunche Hall, UCLA
President, PROFMEX
1242 Lachman Lane, Pacific Palisades, CA, 90272
Tel. cell (310) 454-8812, office 206-8500, Fax: (310) 454 3109
E-mail: wilkie@ucla.edu

Jesús Arroyo Alejandre, Professor and Dean, School of Economics
University of Guadalajara, Jalisco, Mexico
Tel: (011-52-33) 36-33-54-45
E-mail: jesusarr@cucea.udg.mx

Richard Weiss, UCLA Professor of U.S. History
UCLA Bunche Hall 7256, 405 Hilgard Ave, Los Angeles, CA 90095
Tel. (310) 825 1779
E-mail: rweiss@history.ucla.edu

Carlos Alberto Torres, UCLA Professor of Education
Director, UCLA Latin American Center
UCLA, Bunche 10343, 405 Hilgard Avenue, Los Angeles, CA 90095-6859
Tel. (310) 825-4571, Fax (310) 206 6859
E-mail: torres@gseis.ucla.edu and/or CATNOVOA@aol.com

Iván T. Berend, UCLA Professor of East Central European History
Director, UCLA Center for Eastern Europe and Russian Studies
UCLA, 6343 Bunche Hall, 405 Hilgard Ave, Los Angeles, CA 90095
Tel. (310) 825 1178
E-mail: iberend @history.ucla.edu

Ana Torres-Bower, Professor of Philosophy
Former Dean of Social Sciences
Cerritos College
11110 Alondra Blvd.
Norwalk, CA 90650
Tel: (562) 860-2451 Ext. 2778
TorresBower@cerritos.edu

Ronald E. Hellman, CUNY Professor of Sociology
Director, CUNY Center for Science and Society in the Americas
City University of New York
365 Fifth Ave, New York, NY 10016
Tel. (516) 477-4011
rhellman@suffolk.lib.ny.us

Statism, It's Recurring Cycles In Mexico And Romania

OLGA MAGDALENA LAZIN

If you liked this book, read also "*Decentralized Globalization & Antiglobalization*".

www.ingramcontent.com/pod-product-compliance
Lightning Source LLC
LaVergne TN
LVHW040137080526
838202LV00042B/2939